I0074639

THE
ENTREPRENEUR'S
LEGAL
PLAYBOOK

NAVIGATING
THE PITFALLS
THAT CAN
DESTROY YOUR
BUSINESS

PARAG L. AMIN, ESQ.

© 2026 Parag L. Amin

All rights reserved. No portion of this book may be
reproduced, stored in a retrieval system, or transmitted in any
form or by any means - electronic, mechanical, photocopy,
recording, scanning, or other - except for brief quotations
in critical reviews or articles, without the prior written
permission of the publisher.

Published by Parag L. Amin
ISBN: 979-8-9996373-0-7

LEGAL DISCLAIMER

Please note this book was written to provide general
educational information about important legal concepts, but
it is not legal advice. Reading it does not create an attorney-
client relationship with me or my law firm. Every situation
is unique and laws vary from state to state, so before you put
any ideas into action, make sure to check in with an attorney
licensed in your state who can guide you based on your specific
circumstances. If you would like assistance or have questions
about your legal matter, you are welcome to contact my law
firm to explore whether we may be a good fit to help you.

CONTENTS

CHAPTER 1

The Hidden Danger in Going It Alone

My parents immigrated from India to the United States in search of the American Dream—the dream of a brighter, more promising life and future. They settled in New York, which is where I was born. When I was three years old, in furtherance of that American Dream, my parents invested their life savings in a store in Florida, moving our family from New York to Florida. They believed that entrepreneurship held the key to unlocking a better life and future. After all, there's a reason why entrepreneurs from all over the world want to come to the United States to start their businesses.

After we moved to Florida, I hardly saw them because they were usually at the store eighty plus hours per week trying to make it succeed. During that time, I spent my days with my grandmother or at school, only occasionally going to the store because those were the days when people were allowed to smoke indoors, and my parents did not want me around that environment.

After a couple of years of working tirelessly in pursuit of their American Dream, the Florida tax authority suddenly came knocking on the door, claiming that my dad owed over two hundred thousand dollars in unpaid sales taxes.

"There has to be some kind of mistake," he said. "This doesn't make any sense. We don't even make that kind of money here, and I have receipts showing that I paid my sales taxes."

The taxing authorities told him there was no mistake. They clarified that the company had not paid its sales taxes for years before my dad took over. What my dad did not know was that when he bought the entity (i.e. the company) that owned the store, he had bought the unpaid tax liabilities along with it. He had bought all its debts, including the massive unpaid taxes, which were now his. The taxing authority gave him and my mom the ultimatum of either paying the unpaid sales taxes or shutting down the store. Because the debt was so high compared to the profits the store generated, my parents made the difficult decision to shut down the store, walking away from their life savings and the thousands of hours of work they had put into pursuing their American Dream.

After that, our family bounced around for about a year as my father tried to find his footing as an entrepreneur, but he had a young family, and he was unable to find something quickly enough to support himself and his relatively young family. So, he ended up getting a W-2 job, going back to the same factory that he had left to pursue his dream of entrepreneurship.

Unfortunately, because of the significant loss he took, my dad saw choosing a W-2 job as more stable and less risky than entrepreneurship, but I personally believe that being an entrepreneur can be one of the most stable, rewarding, and fulfilling opportunities one could have in life, as well as one of the most challenging. However, the key to success in entrepreneurship is having what my dad did not have: the right guidance. He did not have someone guiding him along the path, and he did not know who to turn to for help when he ran into trouble.

My father's experience is what inspired me to become a lawyer. I did not want what happened to my dad to happen to my family or someone I cared about. I was also determined from a young age to become an entrepreneur myself, to succeed along the journey, and to help others succeed along theirs. That is what my law firm and I do. This is also the "why" behind writing this book. I wanted to write a guide that would protect other entrepreneurs from what happened to my father.

The Importance of Having the Right Guidance

I learned at a relatively young age that it's critical to look into every detail of what you choose to do (what we call "due diligence" in legalese) and to have the right guidance.

As an entrepreneur, you're often trying to figure out a lot of things on your own. I would venture to say that most entrepreneurs probably come from families where they're the first entrepreneur in the family, so there's no one to advise them.

So, while they're trying to figure out a lot of things on their own, they don't know what they don't know. There are things they are aware of that they don't know, but they can adjust for that by seeking guidance or researching answers on their own. However, they can't see their blind spots, and often, it's those very blind spots that destroy businesses and wipe away entrepreneurial dreams.

So, in my dad's example, what he didn't know is that when you buy a company or an entity, if you don't structure it correctly by forming a new company and only buying assets, you're buying all of its debts and obligations. So, if the person who owned it before you didn't do everything that they were supposed to do, such as paying vendors or paying taxes, those liabilities become yours.

I wrote this book to help people find out what they don't know at all. Because from hard-won experience, I know people usually find out what they didn't know when it comes knocking on their door, asking for everything they have.

That's what happened to one of my clients. She had worked most of her adult life as a housekeeper, but eventually, it got to the point where her health deteriorated, and she couldn't physically do the work anymore. So, she started her own housekeeping business.

One of the things that was challenging for her as a housekeeper was the expense of having to drive to somebody's house. She'd have to pay for the gas and to maintain the car, and that was a big expense on a housekeeper's wages.

So, she decided she would provide company cars for her housekeepers to use when driving to and from the homes. Because she wished she'd had that herself.

A couple of years after she had started the business, she got a letter from a lawyer representing some of her ex-employees. It said that she had violated numerous employment laws, including failing to pay all of their time worked and failing to pay overtime wages.

She had been telling her employees, "If you have to be at the job site by 9:00 a.m., come to my house by 8:00 a.m. to pick up one of the company vehicles." But she didn't pay them starting at 8:00 a.m.—she paid them starting at 9:00 a.m. when they got to the job site. That's a big no-no in California.

The state of California is far more protective of consumers and employees than they are of business owners, and the consequences for getting it wrong as a business owner are dire. So, not only did she owe her employees back wages, she owed them waiting time penalties and their attorney's fees. And because California's laws allow the owner to be held personally responsible for all unpaid wages and penalties, all of the client's personal assets were at stake due to these claims—even though she was doing business through her corporation, which she had formed to protect her personal assets.

It wasn't the vast majority of employees that were complaining; it was really just two ex-employees. But under the law, her exposure over those two years she was out of compliance was for hundreds of thousands of dollars due to the penalties and attorney's fees, putting her at risk of losing both her business and her home.

She came to us after receiving the demand letters. Fortunately, we were able to negotiate a favorable resolution for her that ended up saving both her business and her home.

This is a perfect example of someone not knowing what they didn't know. She had no idea that California's laws required this. She hadn't talked to anybody about it. To her, what she did just seemed intuitive and right. She wanted to be nice and make life easier for her employees by letting them use the company vehicles, but it didn't occur to her that she'd have to pay them for time that they wouldn't have been paid for if they'd used their own cars.

That lack of knowledge almost cost her everything that she had worked her entire life to obtain.

In this book, I'll explain things you need to know. I'll tell you what to expect so you are able to prepare. I will teach you how to avoid the mistakes that can destroy your business and offer tips and strategies to handle potential business legal problems.

As a child, I had no way to save my parents' business. But through this book, I may be able to save yours.

CHAPTER 2

How Business Has Changed

The Industrial Revolution transformed the world. It affected everything—economics, social organization, business, and pleasure. Some people embraced the new reality while some people fought against it, but few could ignore the change.

In our modern age, the Internet ushered a similar revolution, which once again evolved the way we live, work, and play. Because of the Internet, business today moves much faster than ever before. We can instantaneously send emails, documents, videos, and images across a state, a country, or around the world. It also allows you to start a business that can transact with people worldwide.

So, this revolution has created many new opportunities and business models. Starting a multi-million-dollar business used to require extensive capital for marketing, employees, and products. Now, you can create an e-commerce store or get paid to promote products or services with only an idea, a laptop or phone, and an internet connection.

Unlimited Leverage: How the Internet Turns One into Many

Some people have managed to start multi-million-dollar businesses with nothing but a cellphone. One of the best examples of that is the rise of the influencer.

Pre-Internet, the ability to reach massive numbers of people was limited to traditional media companies with a lot of resources. Influencers were movie stars, world-renowned scientists, politicians, or famous musicians.

But now you can take a video on your phone, upload it to the Internet, and potentially have it seen by thousands or hundreds of thousands of people. And some people are able to use their charm, skills, and ability to connect with an audience to make millions of dollars a year as influencers—even children as young as three or four years old.

Once you're established as an influencer, you can quickly make decisions about what to promote or how to pivot your business without the need to deal with a stringent approval process. This means you can create content at record rates.

I work with a number of influencers, so during the Hollywood strikes of 2023, I was asked to write an article for the prestigious legal publication *The Daily Journal* about how the strikes were affecting influencers.

The answer is that influencers were far less affected than those working for traditional media companies, because they exist outside of a world that requires screenwriters, camera operators, and actors. They were able to simply continue on as usual because they could rely on themselves to create the content they needed to stay in business. They did not need teams of screenwriters. They did not need an extensive production or editing team. All they needed was their phone and Internet connection to record, edit, and upload their sponsored content to their millions of followers around the globe.

The Global Neighborhood

The Internet has made it much faster to grow a business by increasing your reach. You can potentially reach billions of people with a single post, and this is the first time in history everyone has that ability.

This means you also have the possibility of a much broader customer base. Previously, if you offered marketing services, you would look for local customers. You would canvass the companies or businesses in your area and let them know that you're open for business. You might set up meetings and drive across town to talk about them. Only the largest agencies could have a real national presence, and they were generally located in major media centers.

Now, your marketing agency can have a client anywhere in the world. Working with people you will never meet living thousands of miles away is not just possible—it's common.

Of course, at the same time, your competition can be anywhere. If you're a plumber, you're still competing with the other plumbers in your city or village. But if you're a marketer, you could lose business to someone far away.

Business at Light-Speed

Business just moves much faster now. We communicate faster and make connections more quickly. The speed of money has accelerated, with people able to make payments and investments and transfer money instantly.

People have become millionaires within weeks or months, which is something that has never happened before in history. Even instant millionaires, like oil barons, might have spent months or years prospecting first. Now, we've seen children become rich opening toys on YouTube—or someone's drunken viral comment has allowed them to sell their own cryptocurrency because it's worth hundreds of millions of dollars.

This speed can also allow controversies to rise and spread much more quickly. Companies like Bud Light have been massively damaged by boycotts in a way that would be almost impossible without social media.

Because of the Internet, there are bigger ups to doing business, but also bigger downs. You just have to be careful how you play it.

The Dark Side of the Digital Age

The ease and speed of sharing information creates fantastic new business opportunities and new ways to run a business. But while the opportunities are many, they are arguably matched by all the new pitfalls that unwary business owners may encounter.

So, let's take some time to talk about some of the biggest pitfalls to watch out for in today's Internet Age.

Cyber Vulnerability

One of the great dangers to businesses in the digital age is cybercrime. When data only existed in a physical file room, a thief would have to gain physical access to it. But when businesses use the Internet to make information available to their team and staff, that opens up many opportunities for hackers. They don't need to break into a data room—if they can hack into your online database, they can access all your files, all your secrets, all your communications.

They don't even have to be in the same country as your business, and it can be difficult to find and hold foreign parties responsible. Cybersecurity has become a huge problem, even for major corporations. If their user data is exposed, they are accused of not properly safeguarding their clients' financial, private, or secure information.

Huge companies such as Yahoo or Microsoft have had their servers blocked by hackers. MGM Resorts spends millions of dollars a year on cybersecurity, yet hackers were able to infiltrate the system of their casino-hotel in Las Vegas, gaining access and locking guests out of their rooms and staff out of their own computer systems. Another casino-hotel, Caesars, paid hackers millions of dollars in ransom in order to continue operating.

As a business owner, you have to be aware of the dark side of keeping all of your information on the cloud. Data breaches can lead to multiple lawsuits or even class action against you and your company if you don't have the proper safeguards in place.

This is why it's so critical to have cybersecurity experts examine the servers where client data is stored and to have cybersecurity insurance of at least one million dollars—ideally multiple times that amount. It's to protect you and your business if there is a cybersecurity breach.

If you have a business space, you know the importance of having insurance to protect against physical threats like fires. But while that's an important precaution, for most businesses, cybersecurity issues are more common than fires.

The cost of dealing with a cybersecurity threat can be massive, ranging from tens of thousands of dollars to millions depending on the size of your company and how sensitive and valuable the information is. Also, the more employees you have, the greater the risk that someone opens or downloads the wrong attachment or file.

If hackers gain access to the information you hold, they can sell it to the highest bidder on the dark web or demand a ransom to restore your system functionality. Once hackers gain control of your or your clients' information, there's nothing to prevent them from coming back again and again and again asking for more money for the same information. Accordingly, the best thing you can do is be prepared before it happens, because afterwards it is too late.

With the increase in the number of unscrupulous actors—combined with the increasing abilities of artificial intelligence to better imitate legitimate emails or even voices of those you know—the issue of a cybersecurity vulnerability is really more about *when* it will occur rather than *if* it will occur.

Your credibility matters, and that can hinge on whether you can safeguard your clients' information from hackers. You need to make sure you're doing everything you can to protect yourself, and cybersecurity insurance is the simplest way to start. You can also consult with your cybersecurity insurance company about basic training and measures you can or should be taking to help protect your company and yourself from hackers.

Breaking the Rules Without Realizing It

In the United States, we have freedom of speech. But that doesn't mean we have freedom from the consequences of that speech. This is especially true if you're running a business, where what you say can be regulated or used against you in litigation.

One thing to look out for are Federal Trade Commission ("FTC") regulations relating to what you can and cannot say about products and services on the Internet.

Before the digital age, marketing was done through advertising in newspapers or magazines, or even on TV. This meant that there were a lot of people involved in getting your message to consumers. Most of the time, entrepreneurs would be working with agencies and people who were familiar with marketing rules and regulations. Those companies often had their own lawyers vetting their statements and ad copy. Even if an entrepreneur created their own ads, they still had to be vetted by newspapers or news stations who often had their own legal staff.

This means that, in the past, most material would be thoroughly filtered before it reached the public.

In the Internet age, a business owner or representative can have a thought and simply pick up the phone and post it—whether it's a message on social media, a photo, or a video. This can be launched into the world instantaneously, without any kind of review process. And since the Internet reaches much further than any news or entertainment publication, you can post something to Instagram or TikTok, and the entire world can see it.

That increased visibility comes with increased scrutiny, which can lead to a lot of potential liability if you're making promises that you shouldn't be making or ignoring FTC rules on disclosing sponsorships, agreements, or kickbacks. That worldwide visibility means more potential regulators and government agencies are able to see what you've posted. Your digital history and track record makes it harder to backtrack missteps.

Undermining Your Own Success

It's not just government regulators that you have to worry about when you take advantage of the Internet's speed in spreading your words instantly across the world. There are also people with potential claims against you and your business.

Some employers will post all sorts of things—whether on their personal social media pages or comments on other people's social media pages—because it's so easy. Sometimes, it's a candid reaction to what's happening in the news, or a late-night unfiltered post. But sometimes, the things they post are offensive, insensitive, or even illegal. And sometimes, these posts wind up being used against them in a court of law.

For example, if you're being sued by somebody for racial discrimination or sexual harassment, and you have made offensive comments that speak to your attitudes towards race or sex, some of those comments can be used against you during a deposition or a trial.

So, it's critical that entrepreneurs be careful about what they post online, send in an email, or say on a podcast. Because the Internet has a long memory, which makes it hard to backtrack from a mistake or misstep. That's why I tell my clients: Before you send an email or post something on the Internet, treat it as if one day it may be read to a judge and jury and used to determine the future of you and your business.

The Endless Sprint: Outpacing Your Competition

Because the Internet moves so fast, businesses today also need to work harder than ever to keep up.

Before the digital age, businesses had more time for pivoting or course correction, but even back then, some failed to realize when they began falling behind.

On my office wall, I have a photograph of the Douglas DC-3 propeller plane. People can see it when they're on a video call with me and often ask me about it.

The DC-3 revolutionized transcontinental travel. It was the first aircraft that made travel across continents accessible to the everyday person. A similar type of plane was repurposed for World War II and D-Day, as well as the invasion of Normandy. The DC-3 was a remarkable piece of equipment that was ahead of its time, and which had both civilian and military use.

The manufacturer, the Douglas Aircraft Company, believed that because they had this amazing, successful plane—nobody could catch up with them. The manufacturer became complacent, refusing to embrace modern technology and changes in its processes, even as Boeing and Airbus kept pushing and innovating.

Eventually, Douglas lost its position as a market leader to those competitors, and by 1967, they were out of business.

This is not an uncommon story. Kodak and Polaroid were huge photography companies that decided digital cameras were just a fad and refused to adapt to what became the new reality of photography. The BlackBerry was the once most dominant phone for all business owners, but it failed to innovate its products and keep pace with the ever-changing technology.

While there have always been cases of companies losing their market position through bad decision-making, it can happen a lot faster now. So, one of the critical things in business is staying ahead, avoiding complacency, and continuing to advance your business in an ever-changing landscape. That's why it's so important that business owners embrace technology and innovation in their businesses, which are evolving faster than ever. However, that desire to keep pace with innovation can also expose you to unknown dangers if they are not properly balanced.

The Dangers of the Unknown

Many entrepreneurs are aware of the need to keep pace with technological innovation, but they aren't always aware of the pitfalls that come with them. Many think, "Well, I should take advantage of every opportunity." But without sufficient thought and foresight, they can be opening themselves up to a lot of potential liability.

As you enter a new space, it is critical that you do a risk-assessment not only from a traditional business analysis, but also evaluating potential cybersecurity threats, along with the regulatory registrations and disclosures that may be required before you go live. For example, there are new requirements for companies to provide and disclose their privacy policies about how they are gathering and using consumer data. There are also new requirements regarding how companies must require consumers to opt in to certain kinds of data collection, along with disclosures that must be made if there's a data breach.

Accordingly, as you enter a new space and strive to keep pace with technological innovation, it's also important that you stay compliant and look into the pitfalls before you launch rather than after. There are guides online that can be helpful for businesses; for example, the Small Business Administration dedicates a portion of their website to legal compliance for small businesses. Each state and county also usually has a source of free legal guides that can provide some guidance about potential pitfalls. Similarly, many law firms including mine publish free blogs and newsletters to help business owners stay ahead of legal compliance issues before it's too late. Take advantage of all of these free resources, which are easily accessible from your home or business because of the Internet.

CHAPTER 3

Business Lawsuit Basics

Small businesses often strive to become larger businesses, because business growth is desirable and often advantageous. But any lawyer can tell you that even though growth is desirable and advantageous, it will also come with lawsuits that must be dealt with as you scale.

Take the case of a couple of guys who started a business helping car rental companies service their fleets, doing what was needed to ensure their vehicles were clean, safe, and could get back on the road again right away.

As they serviced these rental companies, the company started doing well, scaling very quickly into a multi-million-dollar business. This was what they wanted.

But they hadn't put some essential, basic things in place, like proper payroll procedures, personnel, and record-keeping. They had written agreements with their clients, but they were one-sided in favor of the rental car companies and didn't provide any real protection to my clients. Of course, they had not come to me before they entered into the agreements but came to me when there was already a problem.

The Domino Effect

When a business scales very quickly but no one's looking at the admin side, the operations side, or the legal aspect of things, problems begin to accrue without anyone realizing they're happening. It's like a leak behind a wall. You don't realize it in the beginning, but it's there. As it starts to get worse, you will eventually see it. But by the time you see it, it's a much bigger, more expensive problem.

My clients didn't recognize the scale of the issues until multiple problems hit them all at once. Suddenly, they had multiple employment claims and problems involving failed payments from a particular rental car agency, as well as multiple lawsuits hitting them all at once. This happened after the company had already scaled to millions in revenue, so these guys had a lot to lose.

As they'd scaled, they'd needed more help, so they hired a guy to help service the fleets. And then this guy brought in other people that my clients didn't know about, one of whom got hurt when someone was moving a rental car. The car hit a woman who had been brought on by their subcontractor to help service part of the fleet. At that point, the subcontractor disappeared. There were no written contracts with that guy, and he wasn't insured.

The injured woman filed a claim for workers' compensation. But she wasn't covered under their workers' compensation insurance, because she wasn't their employee. She never worked for them directly. They didn't even know who this lady was. So, there was no workers' comp insurance to cover the claim.

Then, she filed a separate lawsuit against them for a personal injury claim. So now, she had two separate claims against them.

But it got worse. Their commercial general liability insurance company said they weren't doing things quite right, so they decided not to cover them in these lawsuits. So, there was no coverage for the workers' comp insurance lawsuit or for the personal injury lawsuit.

Then, the injured woman filed a lawsuit against the rental car agency whose car hit her—and the agreement they had with the agency said that my clients agree to indemnify them for their attorney's fees as well. So now, they were on the hook for this rental agency's attorney's fees and damages, in addition to their own for defending the two lawsuits. Next, the rental agency stopped paying them—because the way they saw it, my clients owed them money. So, the subcontractor was gone, there was no insurance whatsoever, and my clients were footing the bill for all of this.

So, they had a domino effect of problems that led to even worse problems, and they wound up facing multiple issues that hit them sequentially, one thing after another. One lawsuit is very challenging for a business, let alone multiple lawsuits at the same time. This kind of situation can destroy your business.

Growing Pains: The Risks Every Business Faces

There are a lot of things you can be sloppy about when you're very small that you might get away with. But as you grow, things that aren't sewn together will pull apart at the seams. If you're going skydiving, the best time to figure out if your stitches are good is while you're still on the ground, instead of after you've jumped out of the plane.

A lot of entrepreneurship is being at the point where you've already jumped, so you need to make sure that your parachute is robust enough to handle anything you might encounter so you can get down safely.

Now, there's a balance between thinking too much about all the legal stuff and not actually taking action on the business. Some people spend a bunch of time and money on legal matters even though they don't really have a business. Then on the flip side are these guys who have millions of dollars in revenue yet never bother to sit down and consider: What are the things that could go wrong? What are the things that we need in place to help protect us?

It's essential that you put safeguards in to scale efficiently, cost-effectively, and legally. Because as you grow, your exposure grows, and you become a bigger target to potential plaintiffs and their lawyers.

Unfortunately, as your business starts to scale and grow, you may not pay attention to all the potential things that could go wrong, because you already have enough things to worry about. It's hard to make sure you're doing the basic things correctly, much less plan for all the things that might potentially go wrong: legal problems, breach of contract issues, ex-employees who are making claims or threats about potential suits, and actual lawsuits against you and your company. And yet, there can be a cost to ignoring those possibilities.

If my clients had thought through what could go wrong, they would have made sure the guy they hired had insurance coverage of at least a million dollars and named them as an additional insured. They would have had a written agreement to make sure safeguards were in place, like having him name them as an additional insured party on his insurance, in case of a lawsuit coming out of something his people did.

Don't Assume Everyone is on the Same Page

In the rush and excitement of starting a new business, it can be easy to leave T's uncrossed and I's undotted. But these things catch up with you. For example, businesses often fail to spell things out clearly when contracting with vendors, or with agreements that lack deadlines, outlining specific processes for handling unmet deadlines, or specifying objective methods to measure whether or not something has been completed.

Similarly, partner disputes often occur because the partners never sat down and worked out their specific job duties and job descriptions, how much time and money they were required to contribute to the business, or whether they could legally start a competing business.

Working out these details might seem like common sense, but many times, people are so optimistic about their new business venture that they just assume everyone is on the same page and everything's going to work out perfectly.

When agreements are not put into writing, complete with clear objectives and metrics, there are inevitable differences about what was actually agreed to and who is supposed to do what. You and your partner remember conversations differently, or don't remember them at all. This leads to a lot of finger-pointing.

Of course, this is assuming there is anyone involved that was even part of the original conversations. As companies grow, there will inevitably be more turnover, so after a while, you'll have disputes based on agreements negotiated years ago by people who are no longer part of the business.

Unfortunately, when things don't work out as expected, it is always more expensive to fix these unanticipated problems.

If you have a legal dispute and it goes to court, you will see that there are four sides to a story. There's what the plaintiff says happened, what the defendant says happened, what the jury comes to believe happened, and what actually happened. And your outcome will be built from those four competing stories.

So, make sure that you've got your agreements in writing. Make sure they are very specific and contain clear, objective metrics. A simple way of thinking about it is that a good agreement spells out exactly who does what by when and the obligations for all parties involved. In that way, both sides can be held accountable. Don't think you will do this later when your company is bigger and more likely to run into problems. Because by the time you're big enough to think, "I need legal counsel," it may be too late to take the proactive actions that could have protected you early on.

To avoid that, sit down with your lawyer now and talk through any issues or potential pitfalls.

Spell It Out, Write It Down

There's something known as the Pareto Principle, or the 80/20 rule. The Pareto Principle is a general rule saying that about 80 percent of consequences come from 20 percent of potential causes. What this means is, identifying and dealing with that specific 20 percent of causes will ameliorate the majority of your issues.

In this context, this means that 80 percent of your potential problems can be prevented by dealing with 20 percent of the things that are within your control. So, you want to initially focus on the 20 percent that will give you the most bang for your buck.

That 20 percent includes documentation. The first and biggest mistake I see business owners make is not having enough documentation for their processes, their business, and their agreements. You want written agreements with business partners, vendors, contractors, and employees. You want all documentation to state specific metrics and consequences. When you have these documents, the people you work with will be clear on what the expectations are, and you'll be able to easily tell if someone has performed or not performed as expected.

Agreements are also hugely beneficial if an issue ever turns into a legal dispute, because you'll have something that you can show to an arbitrator, jury, or judge that shows clearly what was agreed to. That is far more persuasive than simply saying, "Oh, this is what we had agreed on. Believe me, trust me, just take my word for it." People believe written agreements more than they believe anyone's memory.

When working out partnership agreements, you will have to think through potentially uncomfortable problems and ask hard-hitting questions. This is much easier to do in the beginning, while the problems are still hypothetical and emotions are low. If you try to work out an agreement after a dispute has arisen, you will often find that people become very emotional during the discussion. And the higher the negative emotions, the harder it is to come to an agreement on anything, let alone on everything.

So, you want to think through and discuss the uncomfortable situations while the emotions in any partnership are still neutral or positive. Preparing and creating detailed documents is the best way to mitigate your risk in case of future disputes.

Types Of Dispute Resolution

Even if you're well-prepared, legal disputes are almost inevitable. If they happen, you'll need to decide on a method for handling those disputes.

Most legal disputes will be resolved either through litigation or through alternative dispute resolution approaches like arbitration and mediation.

Litigation

Most people, influenced by TV shows like *Suits*, expect that all disputes end up in court. That's not the case, but all the same, let's start with litigation, which is when you file a lawsuit, and it goes to a state or federal public court.

There may be strategic reasons you might choose to file in state court versus federal court, or situations where you have no choice about which court you go to—but that's not something you need much information on as a business owner. Your lawyer should be able to correctly guide you on this.

The process of litigation is that a lawsuit is publicly filed with the relevant state or federal court, and a summons is issued. That complaint and summons are filed by the plaintiff, which then need to be served on the defendants, usually by personally delivering those documents to the defendant—which is known as personal service. Then, depending on where the lawsuit was filed, the defendants have a preset amount of time to respond to the lawsuit. If they don't respond, then a default can be taken against them.

A default is a technical loss where the other side loses, and the plaintiff may be able to collect their judgment because the defendant(s) failed to respond in a timely manner. Alternatively, if the defendant responds to the lawsuit, the lawsuit goes into the discovery phase, where each side gets to ask the other side for information. This phase can include issuing requests for production of documents, asking the other side for documents, requests for admission (i.e., asking the other side to admit certain facts as true), special interrogatories asking the other side specific questions, subpoenas asking third-parties for information they have in their possession, or depositions where you can ask the other side information in real-time.

After discovery, the case may head into trial, which is the part you usually see on TV or movies. That's where the jury is called (if it's a jury trial), and they hear the facts and make a decision.

Alternatively, you can ask for a bench trial, which is where the judge hears the facts and makes a decision, but there is no jury.

Because both sides have a constitutional right to a jury trial, both sides have to agree to a bench trial before it can proceed without a jury. The vast majority of cases—about 98 percent of them—settle before trial. However, exactly when a case will settle varies depending on a number of factors, including the amount of money at issue, the level of disagreement or emotion involved, the number of people involved, how willing each side is to discuss a resolution, and how proactive the lawyer(s) representing the parties are in getting the case to a point where a resolution can be discussed.

As a business owner, what is most important for you to know is that once you go into litigation, everything you've said or done may potentially be used against you in the case. This includes emails and text messages that you've sent and whatever you've posted on the Internet. As I've mentioned before, I tell my clients to treat everything they send, transmit, or put out there into the universe as if one day they might be presented to a judge or jury. These things can really come back to haunt you if a case goes into litigation.

I was involved in a lawsuit where the other side had sent a bunch of inappropriate messages to my client. These weren't the kinds of messages that you would want to share with your family, and there's no need to get into the details of what was said.

The other side claimed that they'd been joking—it was just locker room talk; they hadn't been serious when sending them. But they were things that would be terrible to say regardless of whether or not you were joking, so they were very damaging.

The other side simply could not risk these messages being put in front of a judge or jury. This was especially true because trials are public—members of the public can come see them, and for the most part, look at exhibits and documents, which are filed in the case as public record.

The other side didn't want to risk embarrassment, so because of that and other things we had discovered, they ended up settling the case with very favorable terms for my client.

Things might have turned out differently if not for those text messages. There were a lot of disputes between the parties regarding the terms of an agreement that hadn't been drafted very well. So, if they hadn't been so concerned about those messages reaching the public, it would have been a trickier case for us.

There are drawbacks to litigation. It is time-consuming and often expensive. For example, in California, you might wait a year-and-a-half, two years, or more before your case goes to trial, depending on which county you're in and how full the court docket is. Not all states take that long, but it's not a short process.

Once the trial finally starts, it can take a while to get to a resolution. You'll have the scheduling conflicts of public courts with limited resources and judges with many other cases. That can limit how much time you get in court each day to be able to argue your case.

You can have cases that can go on for months once they get to trial. So, the full litigation process can potentially go on for several years.

Mediation

There are alternatives to litigation or options to try resolving a case during litigation if you want to try for a quicker resolution. One method is mediation, which involves taking your dispute to a private mediator.

The mediator is usually either a practicing or retired lawyer, or a retired judge paid by those who have a dispute. The mediator listens to each side's story and helps them come to a resolution. They're a little like a guidance counselor who sits down with each side separately, asking them what the problem is and who started the fight, and what can be done to get things resolved.

The mediator goes back and forth, usually between two or more rooms depending on how many parties there are, to discuss with each side what their contentions and problems are, as well as what they might be willing to accept or do to get the matter resolved.

Unlike litigation, this is a private process done out of the public eye. Whatever is said at mediation is confidential—you're not allowed to share it with anybody, and nothing revealed there can be used later in a lawsuit.

This is the only way to make sure everyone can be candid in their conversations about what happened, how it happened, and what their position is. They won't be as candid if they worry that anything they say will come back to haunt them if mediation doesn't resolve the dispute.

In mediation, the mediator's goal is to help all parties come to a resolution they can all agree on. The mediator cannot impose any resolution—it's ultimately the decision of the disputants. However, something to keep in mind at mediation is the decision is not binding unless or until a settlement agreement is signed. That is why if you are attending mediation, it is critical that you get something in writing and signed before you leave; if you don't, then mediation privilege will prevent you from discussing the fact that you reached a verbal agreement, and it won't be enforceable.

Arbitration

The other alternative to litigation is arbitration. Like mediators, an arbitrator is a practicing or retired lawyer or, most typically, a retired judge. They act as both judge and jury in your case, and you pay them an hourly rate for the work they do, such as reviewing briefs, making decisions, and listening to evidence at trial.

Arbitration is similar to litigation in that the arbitrator makes the ultimate decision on the case just as a judge would, and participants are required to do as he says. But you can usually get a faster resolution, since the arbitrator isn't stuck with a random docket of assigned cases and has more say-so on who will decide your case. On the other hand, while you will have more confidentiality than in litigation, it won't be as complete as in mediation. For example, the way the case is decided is not necessarily confidential.

One advantage of arbitration is that you and the other side can choose your arbitrator. This means that if you have a dispute requiring a specialized kind of knowledge, you can pick an arbitrator who has that knowledge. In state or federal court, on the other hand, you are typically stuck with the judge regardless of their level of experience and expertise, which means you may have to educate them on the relevant laws.

In litigation, you do have some limited opportunities to be able to strike one judge and pick another judge, but you have much less freedom in picking your judge than you would in arbitration.

Arbitration also comes with more of a VIP level of treatment in terms of how and when your cases and motions are heard. Typically, your arbitration hearing date is set within six to eight months of filing. Your discovery process, which is the process through which you get information from the other side, is usually shorter and a lot more restricted. This can save costs on both sides, but it can also have the consequence of limiting the amount of information you can get from the other side to build your case.

You are also able to go to the arbitrator much more frequently than you would a judge. If you have a problem in the discovery process, such as the other side not giving you information you believe you're entitled to, you get a lot more concierge treatment than when you're paying for the judge's time.

The arbitrator is also a lot more involved in the case than a judge. Whereas the typical judge may have hundreds of cases, arbitrators tend to have just a few. Maybe one or two, maybe as many as ten, but nothing near the caseload of a public judge who usually has hundreds of cases at once. So, the arbitrator is paying more attention to your problems and can resolve issues more quickly.

Another notable difference between arbitration and litigation is that in arbitration, the opportunities for appeals are far more limited. When someone loses a lawsuit in public court, they'll probably file an appeal. However, you have almost no chance of appealing an arbitrator's decision, even if they get the facts wrong or the law wrong.

There are certain ways that you can disqualify an arbitrator's decision, such as proving a failure to disclose certain conflicts of interest. However, it's best to just assume that you probably won't be able to appeal, and if you do appeal the decision, it will probably be upheld.

Arbitration gives you speed and accessibility, but if the arbitrator gets it wrong, it stays wrong. So, that's a trade-off to be aware of.

Better Agreements Equal Better Protection

One of the things that litigation, mediation, and arbitration have in common is that if you have well-drafted legal agreements addressing the possibility of your current dispute, you are in a much stronger position to win your case. So, don't leave this important step until it's too late.

It is helpful to clarify in your written agreements ahead of time what venue you want to use for arbitration, including the place and company, along with the rights to discovery. Your attorney should be able to assist you with thinking through these issues, as they can become more complex. However, some considerations are whether you want to allow broad discovery, which can be more expensive for both sides but can also ensure you have the full opportunity to get all the information you may want from the other side.

Also, the better you define the rights, responsibilities, and timelines of various obligations in your agreement, the easier it will be for the arbitrator to make a good decision on what should have happened. Otherwise, when the agreement is vague, the case gets wrapped up in disputes about what the actual agreement was versus trying to resolve the actual dispute.

Vague starts and obligations will almost always lead to bigger, more expensive problems down the road. So, do your future self a favor and think about the issues ahead of time using the frameworks that are discussed in this book—because if you want better protection, you want to draft a better agreement in the first place.

CHAPTER 4

Partner Problems

Once when I was in trial for a client's case, I got my client's partner—who was on the other side of the litigation—to admit that he had taken money out of their business's bank account at an ATM in a casino because he needed cash for casino chips. He testified that he thought this was a reasonable business expense because running the business was so stressful that he needed to blow off some steam.

Many people in the courtroom laughed or shook their heads, including the judge.

Business expenses are just one item that can lead to partner disputes. Such disputes are common, even if that partnership is made up of family members, romantic partners, or friends.

The common denominator of all disputes is that people will be people. Which is why it's important to establish the rights and responsibilities of partners right away, laying them out in a formal written document, including how and why money can be used or spent.

Of course, no one thinks to write down "don't gamble company money in a casino" in a partnership agreement, because really, that should be a given. But not all disputes are that straightforward.

Plenty of business expenses are more reasonable than gambling to blow off steam. If you have a company car, you'll probably be allowed to use company funds for gas and maintenance. But are you allowed to use it as a personal vehicle? If yes, who pays for that gas and that portion of the insurance? What happens if the company vehicle gets into an accident during personal use, and who is responsible for any increases in insurance premiums resulting from personal use of the company vehicle?

If you're traveling for work, can you fly first class? Is there a limit to per diem expenses for meals and other expenses? Is the sky the limit for hotel expenses, or should you keep costs down? Don't rely on "common sense," because partners may have a different idea of what common-sense, reasonable business expenses are.

For example, we represented a business owner whose partner was running personal expenses through the business, like large electronics, vehicle purchases, and a housekeeper. While my client was doing everything by the book, her business partner wasn't taking the business as seriously and felt he should get to enjoy the fruits of his labor, even if doing so was jeopardizing the business.

They ended up in litigation. But there wasn't a clear partnership agreement setting out what expenses they were and were not allowed to take out of the business, when they were allowed to run any kind of expenses through the business, and what kind of approval processes were needed for such expenses. Those decisions were left to the partner's highly subjective feelings on what was appropriate.

You don't want business expenses to be in the eye of the beholder—you want everything spelled out. Otherwise, you'll just have arguments about whether expenses are too high, because one person's reasonable expense is another's exorbitant extravagance.

You can save yourself a lot of trouble by simply putting specific things into writing, such as expense limits and approval processes, as well as how frequently these limits and determinations can be revisited for the purposes of increasing the amount.

Talk About Compensation Even Before There is Money for Salaries

It might seem strange to start a business and never talk about what the owners are to be paid, but it's not uncommon. People start a business, and nobody really talks about salaries.

Ignoring something that important would be strange in other endeavors. Imagine someone told you they were building a house. You ask how big it's going to be, and they say, I don't really know. How many rooms will it have? Not sure. Do you have a blueprint? No. So, you're just going to start building this house without a plan? Yes, I'll just start building it and see where it goes.

Even if you didn't have a background in construction or architecture, you wouldn't build a house without a blueprint. But when people build a business, they often don't have a blueprint at all.

So, people start a business and never discuss salaries. And what can happen is, you will have people doing work for the business, and there may be one partner who's doing more than the others or has more roles than the others, and is thus putting in more hours than the others—they then feel entitled to be paid more for all that work. So, they start taking extra money out of the business as compensation or expenses that have never been discussed, and it leads to a lot of friction.

And all of that can be solved by having these discussions early on. What are you specifically going to be doing for the business? Will you be compensated for it? How much? How often?

That conversation often doesn't happen at the beginning. Talking about salaries isn't that exciting, especially when there's not enough money to actually pay anyone. Partners say, why are we taking time to talk about salaries now, when we aren't making enough money?

Instead, you focus on growing the business. Then, as the business grows, you're spending all your time servicing all that business, so there's no time to talk about salaries.

It takes a lot of intention and planning to create a business blueprint. If you don't create that attention and take the time to plan, then it just slips away from you, because there's always going to be other stuff that makes demands on your time and your attention. And you probably will never get to the more important things that might destroy your business or create issues, because you haven't intentionally thought about them. So, they're not realistically going to come up to be discussed until they're an actual problem. Remember, it is easier to plan ahead and solve hypothetical problems now than to wait until they are actual problems and try to solve them later.

Division of Labor

Business expenses aren't the only source of disagreement. There are many cases where partners disagree on what they should be doing for the company.

For example, I had a partnership case where my client was the partner who was very good at running the business operations. He kept everything running extremely well and made sure all the work got done.

The other business partner was good at marketing and bringing in business, which was the only part of the business she was responsible for.

In the beginning, this seemed like a good way to divide the work, so they didn't bother to formally work out each partner's responsibilities. But over the next few years, the business became successful and began generating a lot of money. The business partner who was doing the marketing but not doing any of the day-to-day work had a lot of freedom and was doing more or less whatever she wanted.

Meanwhile, the business partner responsible for operations was servicing all of the business, dealing with the staff and human resources issues, and handling everything required to keep the business running. This was taking up a lot of his time, and he felt like he was getting the short end of the stick.

So, the partners had a major disagreement about this.

Ultimately, we negotiated a buyout where my client got paid a lot of money for his ownership in the business. But it took a decent amount of time to negotiate what the buyout looked like and what he was legally allowed to do once he walked away, like whether or not and where he could start a competing business. Many details needed to be talked through, and they took longer now that the business was worth a lot of money since each partner wanted a lot more money to walk away with than the other wanted to pay since the business was doing well.

The root of this dispute was simply that the partners had never discussed what hours each partner would be expected to work when the business became more successful. The partner who did all the marketing considered herself to have a pure marketing role and felt she wasn't required to help in any way with operations or staffing. She felt that those things were her partner's job.

This is how things had been done since the business was started, even though there was nothing in writing indicating that this was how the work would be divided up.

While we were able to get a favorable resolution without litigation, things could have turned out differently in court. When it comes to relationships and contracts, if the parties differ on what the actual agreement was, many times courts and juries will look at the patterns and practices to help determine what the de facto agreement was. They could have decided that the history of the business would be in favor of the business partner who only did marketing, while my client was entirely responsible for operations.

These two could have saved themselves a whole lot of money, trouble, and headaches had they simply discussed everything at the beginning and written down exactly what was required from each of them.

Fair Shares

Ultimately, the disagreement with those partners was over whether each was doing their fair share. And what is considered a person's fair share can be very subjective. One person might think they're doing a lot while their partner is of the opinion that they're actually doing very little. Each person sees it from their own perspective, and it can be very challenging for a partner to see things from the other's perspective.

When the amount of work required is left up to the partner's subjective feelings, you set yourself up for failure. Instead, create some objective metrics that can be used to measure whether each person is doing the amount of work expected of them.

Second Businesses

Sometimes a partner is not devoting as much time to their business as their partner thinks they should because they have started another business. It might be a business that competes directly with the partner's business, or it might be something unrelated, but either way it is taking away their time, attention, and energy.

That is something that can be addressed in a partnership agreement. Are partners allowed to start competing businesses or engage in other business enterprises? If so, when and how? Are they required to put a certain amount of time, energy, or effort into the business you share, or achieve a certain level of results before they can start something new?

I highly recommend having objective metrics in place so you can easily determine whether somebody is holding up their end of the business. Otherwise, if a partner starts a second business, they will inevitably argue that they were allowed to do so because there was nothing in any partnership agreement or in any discussion with you that prohibited them from doing so.

Decisions You Don't Make May Be Made for You

Going into a business without signing an agreement doesn't necessarily mean you won't be subject to a set of rules. They just won't be the rules you choose.

For example, in California, if you form a general partnership, which just means you're going into business together, that partnership will be governed by the Revised Uniform Partnership Act. There are specific rules that you default to if you don't have a written agreement. For example, partners are supposed to split profits and losses equally. And they're each completely responsible for the partnership's debts—meaning they're jointly responsible together for the full amount, and they're separately responsible for the full amount if one of them is unable to pay.

If you form your business as a corporation or an LLC, there will be different requirements, and you will be governed by different laws. But whether you're forming a general partnership or creating an entity like an LLC or a corporation, the best thing to do is to create your own rules in terms of how you want it to be governed. Legal defaults will often not do what you want.

Successful businesses aren't IKEA furniture—you can't just grab one off the shelf and hope it will be exactly what you need. The same is true of generic contracts, which often fail to have provisions for your specific type of business and circumstances. For an agreement to protect you, it needs to anticipate the actual issues you're likely to have.

Life and Death Issues

Life can be messy, and partnership agreements can be used to protect your business from the complications of marriage, divorce, and death.

People often don't want to believe that their marriage is fragile enough to shatter. But since almost half of all marriages in the U.S. end in divorce, it's dangerous to make assumptions about which side of that line you'll wind up on.

If you or your partner gets a divorce, this can bleed into your business. This is especially true if your business is located in a community property state such as California, where unless they have some kind of prenuptial/postnuptial agreement, your business partner's spouse technically owns half of what your business partner owns.

This means you could be subject to a family court's orders regarding the ownership of your business. The ex-spouse may wind up with an ownership interest in your business, or the business may need to come up with a lot of capital to buy out the quarter-share they now own. If you haven't thought through how you're going to handle a business partner's potential divorce, then this can lead to a lot of turmoil and problems in your business.

Similar issues can arise upon the death of a partner. Once again, you could wind up with a brand-new partner you don't want or for whom you have to negotiate a buyout.

With death, unless there is something in your agreement that allows the partnership or entity to buy back the ownership in the event of death, the deceased's share in the business will be treated like any other piece of property. It's just like inheriting a car, or a grandfather clock, or a dining room table. The person who inherits may lack interest or expertise in the business, but they've got it all the same.

But unlike an inherited object, a business is ongoing, requiring decisions, agreements, and a vision for the future. And when someone with no interest or knowledge in a business is suddenly able to exert control over it, that can lead to a lot of friction, especially when it's somebody who has built the business with their partners or co-owners.

So, it can actually *destroy* a business. Let's say those people are completely unreasonable, and they have no business sense. You can't legally ignore their input, because they have the same stake your partner did.

Serious disability is another thing to plan for. If a partner gets a brain injury, is he still the same guy? Can he actually provide the same kind of value?

Are you all of a sudden deadlocked because you need a certain percentage of votes, or have to unanimously agree on things, but you can't even discuss things with your partner?

Does their family have power of attorney, putting your business at the mercy of someone chosen not for business acumen but for their trustworthiness as a health advocate?

This is why your partnership agreement should be written to specify what happens to a partner's ownership interests in the event of death, disability, or divorce. For example, you can require that either the deceased partner, the spouse, or both have to sell back their ownership interests at a pre-specified price or use some other valuation method such as fair market value. If you don't have this set up, then your business will be at the mercy of interpretation by a third party, such as a judge or jury.

If your business partner is married, and you live in a community property state such as California, make sure that the spouse as well as the partner signs off on the partnership agreement. If they haven't signed that agreement, then during a divorce they could argue that they never agreed to sell their half of their soon-to-be ex-spouse's half. Then, you could find yourself tied up in litigation or an extended dispute. Make sure that you're thorough and diligent, and that both spouses sign off on the agreement.

Keep in mind that if your partner gets married *after* the business is formed, and you and your partner have already signed an agreement, you need to have that new spouse sign the agreement as well.

Things Change, So Be Ready

People's lives and circumstances can change over time, and those changes can lead to partnership disputes. The best time to deal with potential problems is before they occur. So, make sure you and your partners discuss what is expected from each partner and follow that up by creating a legal document with clear written guidelines outlining expectations that include objective metrics about who is supposed to deliver what by when. The sooner this is done, the less subjective disagreements you will have going forward.

CHAPTER 5

Vendor Suits

A vendor suit is when you've hired somebody for yourself or your business, and they're supposed to do something, but they don't do it correctly, or at all. It can also go the other way, where a vendor sues because the client didn't pay them what they were supposed to or failed to pay them in a timely manner.

The most helpful way to avoid vendor suits is to have a written agreement that is clear about who's supposed to do what, when they're supposed to do it, what each side's obligations are, and what the consequences are for not meeting deadlines. You want to include the specifics of how much the client is supposed to pay and when they're supposed to pay it, and the specifics of what the vendor will supply in terms of services, functionality, look, size, features, and everything else. The more specific you can be, the better.

A breach of contract lawsuit is when somebody says the other side didn't do what they were supposed to do, as stipulated in the contract. Often in contract disputes, both sides wind up claiming that the other side has not followed the language of the contract. So, in these cases, it's often necessary to work out exactly what each side was contractually required to do and how that differs from what they actually did.

So, the clearer the contract is about what they're supposed to do, the easier it is to help resolve the problem. Having clarity, having it in writing, and making sure everybody's on the same page is important throughout a client-vendor engagement. If you have a dispute, explaining or confirming in writing what conversations you're having is also helpful, regardless of what kind of contract or issue it is.

If you've got a breach of contract, ideally, you want to try to resolve it as quickly and efficiently as possible. But what that means in your case can vary in terms of how to best resolve it.

Breach of Contract Is Not Always Intentional

Often in a breach of contract dispute, each side points at the other as the one who isn't properly fulfilling the terms of the contract.

For example, I had a client whose business washed vehicles for all of the major car rental companies. My client said that one of those companies had not paid a series of invoices. But while he contended that they hadn't properly paid him for his work, the other side's contention was that they had.

So, contractually, the invoices were supposed to be paid within thirty days of being submitted. But contractually, the invoices also had to be submitted in a certain way. But, neither side was doing exactly what was in the agreement. Each side was doing something slightly different from what was in the agreement. Invoices were being submitted, and payments were being issued, but not in the way the contract specified.

At first, this seemed like it was working, but eventually, there were a number of unpaid invoices, even though the contract had been written to avoid unpaid invoices. So, because the invoices were not submitted in the form required by the contract, the payments were not issued clearly enough to comply with the contract either. That resulted in a huge misunderstanding about what invoices and work had been paid and not paid.

My client said they hadn't been paid for the work they had done. The other side said they had paid for a lot of this work, but there were problems with the way the invoices were submitted.

Now, when this dispute started, one of the first decisions both sides had to make was whether to keep doing business together while they worked through the issues. Should they simply stop doing business together? Or would it make sense to continue doing business while the lawsuit proceeds? Ultimately, they decided that it made financial sense for them to continue to work together, figuring out what was going on with the unpaid invoices at the same time. So, they went back and forth about the payments, totaling them up, dealing with contentions about things being resubmitted, rebilled, double billed, or sent in correctly—all the time continuing to do business and make money together.

Sometimes it makes sense to continue working with somebody you have an issue with. Not always, but it happens. There have been lawsuits between Microsoft and Apple, where they're still on each other's boards, still buying and selling things with each other in spite of suing each other. Same thing with Samsung and Apple. Sometimes it makes business sense for them to continue to cooperate. So, you can segregate the disputes and issues while continuing to do business.

When making these decisions, it's important to have a good, sensible attorney who has the emotional intelligence to understand what good business is. Because if you've got an attorney who goes in there like a crazy, blind bulldog—who is just aggressive about everything without thinking it through or seeing what's really going on—then it can complicate or destroy the business relationship, even when it would make financial sense to keep it despite the dispute.

It was important to recognize that in this case, where no one was intentionally breaching the contract or trying to harm the other party. There was just a lot of confusion that needed to be ironed out.

When the Vendor Screws Up

When vendors supply services, they make promises about what they're going to do and, sometimes, even what the outcome should be. But it's important to understand that if those promises aren't in the contract, then it's not a breach if they don't deliver on those promises.

I had a client who learned this the hard way when her e-commerce site crashed—on Black Friday. She had a big e-commerce and retail operation selling cosmetics, and Black Friday was a big day for her. She had hired a website company to redo the backend, because they persuaded her that an upgrade would mean the site would work faster and more efficiently, increasing her sales by up to 30 percent. They showed her all this data to that effect, and so she hired them.

But after they built out the backend, the website crashed on Black Friday for the first time ever. She lost millions in sales. So, she filed a lawsuit. She said something to the effect of, "You guys didn't do what you said you were going to do. You said you were going to build a better website, but it wasn't better like you promised. My website's never crashed before. So, this is your fault, and you guys owe me all of the money I lost because of this crash."

So, there were issues that we had to work through about whose fault it really was that the site had crashed. The client said it was the vendor's fault. The vendor said it was the client's fault—that they weren't supplied with certain necessary information.

The challenge was helping figure out what the prior considerations and conversations were about what this company was supposed to do for her, and what it was supposed to build out. To figure this out, we had to go back through everything and understand what the agreement and conversations were regarding the website build-out.

Unfortunately, the contract that the client had signed—before I was involved—specifically disclaimed any and all representations and warranties regarding the website, as well as limiting the consequential damages if the site didn't work properly. Those sorts of disclaimers and limits are enforceable in these kinds of contracts.

So ultimately, the client didn't have a claim, because the promises they made weren't in the contract, and the contract protected them rather than my client. All I was able to do was get her money back, which was maybe thirty to fifty thousand dollars. So, she lost millions. And ultimately, she had signed this contract, and there was nothing that could be done about it.

That's why it's so important that whoever's drafting the agreement actually understands the business. Because you could have a contract that looks good and formal, but the reality is it doesn't cover all the aspects or mechanics of the deal, so it may not serve your purposes.

Having a good contract is a part of understanding what the actual terms are. Ultimately, if there's a dispute and the point of disagreement isn't included in the contract because somebody didn't think through the logistics of the deal, then it can create problems and issues.

When the Vendor Overuses Leverage

Contracts often hold provisions that allow vendors or clients to take certain actions during a dispute. And if those contracts allow extreme actions, there is some chance that one party will go for the most extreme option.

This happened to my clients, who had a shipping and logistics company and kept their materials in a warehouse. When something was purchased, the logistics company would call the warehouse and say, "Pack this up and ship it out."

Part of the agreement that the clients had signed before they came to me pertained to a lien for unpaid invoices. So, there were disputes between my clients and the vendor relating to theft of my client's materials. Electronic and other high-end equipment was being stored there, and the shrinkage was far above the industry average.

So, my clients complained that their stuff was being stolen from the warehouse, and that meant running their business through the warehouse did not make any financial sense. This led to a dispute regarding issues about invoices and charges on those invoices.

So, the warehouse stopped shipping out my clients' materials altogether. The warehouse's lawyer pointed out language in the contract saying the warehouse had a lien over all of my clients' assets if they didn't pay their invoices. There was some language in there that they read as allowing them to pause services—or hold off on shipping—if the warehouse was owed money because the lien is a property right that allowed the warehouse to hold or sell my clients' inventory to be paid.

They said, "We have a lien on this stuff, and we're not going to let you keep selling it and shipping it out if you haven't paid us our invoices."

At this point, the lien was for a little over a hundred grand, but the warehouse was holding up millions of dollars in inventory over it. They wouldn't let the client move or sell anything because of this dispute over what was really a very small amount of invoices. But they said, "We're entitled to this money, and we've got a lien over your equipment if you don't pay it, so we're not shipping out a single thing."

So, I got involved. I warned the warehouse and its lawyer that by holding up millions of dollars in inventory, they were creating damages far in excess of what they claimed they were owed. I said that if they didn't release this inventory ASAP, they would be looking at a lawsuit worth millions of dollars.

That convinced them to start releasing the inventory while we worked things out. They just held the lien to maybe two hundred thousand dollars' worth of inventory—which is what they should have done to begin with. And once we had that agreement, we were able to work through all the issues and come to a satisfactory resolution.

Vendor suits are tricky, because the client/vendor relationship is often an essential part of the business. Clients don't always have good options for replacing vendors, and vendors don't want to lose clients, especially big ones, even if there are issues with them.

So, it is in both sides' interests to have a contract that is detailed and full of specifics—and for both sides to document their interactions. In this way, misunderstandings are less likely to arise, and disputes are more likely to be settled quickly and efficiently. Thinking through the potential issues and negotiating a well-drafted contract takes time on the front end, but it will likely save you many multiples of the time and money on the back end if there's an issue.

CHAPTER 6

Client and Customer Problems

Every business wants satisfied customers. But if you're contractually required to satisfy those customers, you may find yourself facing the unsolvable problem of facing a customer who is never satisfied. I had a client who learned that the hard way.

Years ago, my office dealt with a software dispute, representing a software developer whose agreement with their client included vague language stating that the developer would perform to their client's satisfaction. The client would not be required to pay for services until they were satisfied.

My office was not involved in drafting the agreement. I can understand that, in theory, this seemed like a good way to indicate a commitment to customer service, but wherever they got the idea of this open-ended promise, it was the worst legal advice they possibly could have received. A smart lawyer should and would have foreseen the danger that language created.

This contract put my client in an untenable position. They had spent hundreds of extra hours trying to satisfy a client who was impossible to satisfy. They had added and changed features and done a whole lot of extra work that was never a part of the original scope, all at no additional expense to their client. All the expense was borne by my client as they tried to satisfy their client and avoid a dispute based on the terms of their agreement.

Client and customer problems are an unfortunate reality of doing business. People will be people, and you will have disagreements with your clients. That's why it's so important to have a clear understanding, including a formal agreement with objective metrics for measuring success.

Defining "Satisfactory"

In my client's case, the problem was that "satisfaction" is subjective. There was no objective metric being used. It didn't say, for example, that proper completion will require specific features, along with a definition of what a working feature actually would be within the context of the project. Nor did it say that the finished product would support a certain number of users or be able to run a certain number of simultaneous tasks. It didn't give the kind of metrics that would allow an objective third party to come in, look at the work, and say, "Yes, this was done as promised."

Instead, they had the subjective criteria of performing to the other side's satisfaction. And of course, the other side claimed they weren't satisfied and couldn't be satisfied without all these additional features that weren't within the scope of the agreement. And if those features were added, they would not be satisfied because of X, Y, and Z. And when X, Y, and Z were resolved, the client would find other issues that they wanted addressed.

This became an extremely expensive problem for the client to resolve, and this all could have been avoided by having a clear agreement in writing with objective metrics in place.

Ultimately, we were able to resolve this matter. But it cost the client far more money than it would have if they had had a clear agreement in place.

The WDWBW Framework

Client and customer problems come down to the same issues that we've talked about before, which is failing to think everything through ahead of time—for example, what success looks like.

When drafting an agreement, it is helpful to use a "who does what by when" framework—i.e., we will deliver this thing to you, with these features, by this date. You, as the customer, will pay this amount by this date. If the project has multiple milestones, then you can specify the WDWBW for each stage.

The more specific you can get and the clearer you are about roles and responsibilities, the better off you are. You should also work out what will happen if, in spite of your very specific agreement, there is a dispute. You'll want language involving how that is to be mediated.

Clear Timelines

A good customer agreement includes a clear timeline of what will be delivered and by when. This is critical, because otherwise you might have unreasonable clients demanding short turnaround times. They may insist on a 24-hour completion for something you might normally spend a week on, and it could cost you a lot of extra time and money to satisfy that demand. And if you say that's unreasonable, they may insist that it was obvious that they would need it in this amount of time, and then there comes a big back-and-forth about who knew what about the other person's business and what they needed.

If you formally agree to a timeline, then you have an agreement outlining your clear mutual expectations.

For example, we had a dentist client who was building out some space that he had leased from the owner, who happened to be a lawyer.

The dentist ran into all kinds of issues and problems with the construction, so it was taking a while. All of a sudden, my client gets a demand from the landlord telling him, "You need to sign this agreement to complete construction or start paying rent by this date, or I'm going to terminate your contract and your lease."

The landlord was upset, because the agreement the landlord had made with the dentist was very open-ended, including that the client would start paying rent no later than thirty days after construction was complete. But the construction was taking longer than expected.

The problem for the landlord was that the construction had multiple delays, and the end wasn't in sight. There was a whole dispute between the landlord and my client about whose fault that was. My client said there were problems with the building that needed repair. The landlord claimed my client didn't really know what he was doing and was trying to get too many different bids for the same type of project, instead of just getting one or two bids, then starting construction. So, the landlord wanted to change the contract to make it clear when my client would begin paying rent.

I said, "Look, the agreement is the agreement. Now you're insisting that my client change the agreement to his own detriment, without anything new or favorable for him." And I warned the landlord that terminating the contract in violation of the agreement would open him up to a lawsuit for all the time and money my client had put into the space, as well as any additional time and money he put into finding a new place.

I told him, "You signed this agreement. If you've got a problem with these terms, it's not my client's fault—my client is abiding by the agreement and acting diligently. You're a lawyer; you should know better." So, the landlord backed off.

When the original agreement was drafted, the lawyer could have added something saying, "If construction is not complete within six months of signing this contract, the landlord has the right to terminate this agreement." But he didn't.

Setting Some Rules

It's shocking how many people don't read agreements or really care what's in them—they'll just sign whatever. That's why it's helpful to draft an agreement that's more favorable to you. Then, if the other side has a problem with it, they can push back. And if they don't push back, you've got a really nice agreement.

For example, I had a client that was a big-time social media agency focusing on platforms like Instagram and high-end influencers, where people are willing to pay money for a shoutout or a tag of their product. On the high end, influencers can command tens or hundreds of thousands of dollars for that—sometimes even seven figures for a single post.

Agreements were often very specific in terms of how and when money was due, and how much detail was required in posts. And the more sophisticated the party was on the other end, the more detailed it would be. It would say something like, you will post within this five-minute window on these dates using these hashtags. You will not have these things in your background. You will make it seem casual. You will wear something similar to this. The agreements were extremely specific.

As a middleman between the companies and the influencers, my client had to make sure both sides were going to do what was expected. For example, imagine a scenario where payment is due sixty days after achieving a particular milestone. But what if an influencer can't achieve that milestone because they're waiting on something from the company? Should they not get paid because the company didn't hold up its end? What if the company tried to keep to a schedule, but the influencer was difficult to reach?

So, what we did was include some language specifying requirements for reasonable cooperation and timelines about what needed to be provided by whom and by when. Parties needed to respond within a certain number of days to inquiries, requests, and other communications. That precluded somebody just dragging their feet or not cooperating, and then saying, "Well, you guys didn't do this."

Heading Off Trouble

Now, you can't avoid every unreasonable customer. It's impossible. You can try to minimize the chances, but you can't completely eliminate bad customers, no matter how hard you try to get rid of them. So, what you want to do is put some safety mechanisms in place, which address required reasonableness.

For example, we had a client who made packaging for cannabis products, which have been legal here in California for quite some time.

She had delivered some plastic casings to protect products during shipping to a client. But six months later, the client not only refused to pay for them but claimed that they were all defective, and he couldn't use them. My client believed he did use them and simply didn't want to pay her.

The way to head off that kind of issue is to include in the agreement a requirement that, if you've got a complaint about the quality, you've got to let us know within thirty days of delivery. This is especially important if you're dealing with a product that can be damaged by improper storage. For example, I have a client who does tobacco import, but if you store it under the baking sun, it will dry up. So, if a purchaser comes to him six months later and says, "This tobacco was bad," who knows how they stored it?

So, you want to make sure that you've got certain safeguards and time limits in place, again going back to who does what by when. In this case, you also want your agreement to specify complaints be made in writing, so they don't say, "Oh, well, I called."

Getting People to Act Reasonably

Just because you have a contract doesn't mean people will follow it. So, when people aren't complying with an agreement, part of my job is to change that.

When clients ask for my help, I usually tell them I'll start by making a call or sending a letter, and they will say, "Oh, I tried that already." I'll say, "Right, but *I* haven't tried that." Because a call from a lawyer can really grab someone's attention. Many times, clients are very pleasantly surprised—who knew that that would work?

For the most part, people really do want to comply with agreements. The people who lack all integrity and just lie to your face are the minority. So, a lot of disputes arise because something has come up where no one ever discussed it or who would be responsible for taking whatever risk it represented. Nobody really wants to take on additional risk for no reason, but if you can show them how the agreement they signed makes them the responsible party for this surprising development, they will generally agree.

Ultimately, the best way to prevent client and customer problems is to set expectations ahead of time—and to act quickly and proactively when problems do arise.

CHAPTER 7

Employee Problems

An e-commerce store had an employee who just wasn't good at her job. Her job was packing boxes that would be shipped out from the warehouse. But sometimes, she would pack things in the wrong boxes or just didn't pay attention to what she was doing. Not only was she bad at her job, but she also created all kinds of friction and problems with her coworkers—they were uncomfortable around her. So, the company intended to let her go.

But before they got a chance to fire her, she came to them and said that she'd been hurt on the production line and needed to leave to seek medical treatment.

The store thought, "Well, we were going to fire her anyway, so we might as well go ahead and do it now, since she's leaving for the day anyway." So, they told her, "Sure, go to the doctor and get yourself checked out, but don't bother coming back because you don't work here anymore."

Now, it's generally not unlawful to fire someone. But, if you fire someone because they are injured, or because they complained to you about a safety issue, then that's against the law in almost every state. Those situations have to be handled carefully, because it can create huge exposure for the business if they are handled incorrectly.

So, the employee saw an opportunity to file an employment lawsuit, claiming that she was only terminated because she complained about being hurt, instead of because of her poor performance. That's when this company came to me seeking help with the problem.

While this client was already planning on letting this person go, the documentation written up on her wasn't as helpful as I would've liked. They had no formal disciplinary or write-up file on this employee documenting either her poor performance or any discussions with her about her poor performance. Instead, everything was done verbally. Of course, when I discussed this with opposing counsel, he said his client claimed those discussions never happened.

Because of the sparse documentation, the ex-employee's lawyer had an easier time arguing that his client was improperly terminated as a result of her injury rather than her improper performance. Luckily, I was able to get this matter resolved for my client for less than ten thousand dollars—this case could easily have been a six- or even a seven-figure case in California.

However, resolving it was quite difficult, since I did not have any documentation from the client that helped.

Have Proof

It's critical to make sure you're following a formal process for write-ups and termination. These are the kinds of documents that lawyers will examine later if there's a claim of improper termination. And while in California you are allowed to fire employees for any proper reason whatsoever, there are improper reasons—like firing people for their sex, religion, race, or medical conditions—that can open you up to a wrongful termination suit. You need to be careful about how and when you terminate people, because these things can really come back to haunt you.

Even big, publicly traded companies with their own HR departments sometimes completely fumble on this.

I know of a woman who worked in the accounting department of a company like that. She was pregnant and due to give birth soon. Her company was facing issues and needed to strategically lay off some of the people in the accounting department, and she was one of them.

Now, discriminating against someone who is pregnant is a violation of both federal law and state law in almost every state. If you terminate or refuse to hire somebody because they're pregnant, you can be held liable. So, it's important to comply with those laws—and with maternity leave laws that require keeping their position open until they can return to work after their maternity leave is over.

So, when they laid off that pregnant woman, they created a real opportunity for a lawsuit. And it's mind-boggling, because they have an HR department and a law firm that advises them on these things—but somehow, either they didn't have the full context, or they made a rash decision. But if that lady went and sued, there's zero doubt in my mind that that's a multi-six-figure—if not seven-figure-*plus*—case in California.

So, if big companies with lots of resources and information screw this up badly, you can see how a small company without an HR department or regular outside legal counsel can get something like this wrong and inadvertently create a lot of liability.

A simple rule of thumb would be: If you're going to terminate somebody or lay them off, and they can be considered a part of a protected class, you need to be very careful. You are certainly allowed to terminate someone who is pregnant, but you need to be extra careful about having documentation that backs up the need for your actions.

This means you need to know what is considered a protected class where you are. This can include pregnancy, disabilities, medical conditions, race, religion, or in some states, even weight. In California, you cannot terminate or take an adverse employment action against an employee for their political beliefs or activities—I don't know that that's the case in every state, but it's always best to just double-check these things before you lay somebody off or terminate them and tell them the reason they are being terminated.

I think a lot of times what happens is these things build up over time. And then one day, all of a sudden, the company fires that employee. But now, the employee is out of work and looking for a payout to pay their own bills. So, they could very easily go to a contingency fee employment lawyer who decides what violations are clear there and make a claim. As an employer, you'll know it's happening when you get a letter in the mail asking for the former employee's employment file, including all wage and hour statements as well as any and all write-ups. That means the employment lawyer has been hired to look into violations—and if you are in a state like California, they are almost certainly going to find some. So, if you get a letter like that, it's best to call a lawyer as soon as possible in order to put yourself and your company in the best position possible to defend yourselves.

The Importance of an Employee Records

Employee problems often occur because of unclear expectations on both sides. That's why it's so important to spell everything out clearly, including job duties, job descriptions, and key performance indicators for the position with specifics about what success looks like.

Once you have clear expectations and measurable indicators, you need to track and document performance failures and other issues. This way, if you need to fire them, you can show why it was necessary. If you're terminating someone, and you haven't kept good records about how this person was performing, you could be facing a situation where the employee claims they were wrongfully terminated for an illegitimate or invalid reason, such as their race, religion, or something else.

The best thing you can do to prevent this is have written documentation about what is required from the person, as well as clear criteria that lets you track how this person is performing in their role.

Labor laws vary state by state. Since I practice in California, I'm going to focus on the labor laws here. Whatever state you're in, it is very important that you are familiar with—and compliant with—employment laws and regulations.

You should have clear documentation on a problematic employee's job performance, including items like how many hours they're working, and whether they've taken all of their meal and rest breaks. Make sure that if you terminate somebody, you're processing their payroll in accordance with the law. For example, California requires that you offer your employee their check immediately upon termination.

You want to make sure that these procedures are clear to employees and managers. If managers aren't clear on the rules, they may fail to comply with them.

In California, this could lead to a situation where you're personally exposed and liable.

A lot of California business owners don't know that, in California, regardless of whether you have an LLC, an S corporation, or a C corporation, you can be held personally responsible and liable if you don't pay your employees all of their overtime or their wages. Because of the way California law is written, business owners have individual personal liability to their employees for unpaid wage and hour issues, as well as meal and rest breaks. And because of things like time penalties and other interest and fees that get tacked on—such as attorney's fees—they can wind up owing the employee five to ten times more than the unpaid wages.

If you don't keep track of the hours that your employees worked, there can be a de facto presumption that whatever hours the employee claims they worked are correct. Another penalty can get tacked on—and another claim made—if you've failed to keep and provide accurate wage and hour statements and records. And you'll have personal liability and responsibility for these oversights.

The Pros and Cons of the Employee Handbook

Popular opinion holds that a business with employees should have an employee handbook. But I think there are risks to having one that employers should be aware of.

Anytime I've handled the case on the plaintiff's side, the first thing we go through is the employee handbook—to see what the requirements are and what was followed or not followed. Because the lowest-hanging fruit when it comes to an employment suit is when you don't follow your own employee handbook. It's a clear violation.

Usually, the people crafting the employee handbooks are either involved in compliance (so they don't deal with litigation), or on the employment defense side (so they haven't really dealt with the plaintiff side). So, my experience as that rare lawyer who has worked on both sides of employment law—both for the employee and for the employer—gives me a different view than you'll see elsewhere.

What can happen is that someone gets pitched on the importance of having an employee handbook, and then they have one that they haven't looked at or haven't properly followed when it comes to discipline.

The whole idea of the employee handbook is to give an overview of the company and the business, including how certain things work. It can be helpful for outlining things like paid holidays, probationary periods, and so on. But you can also lay those out in a welcome letter, an offer letter, or in the job duties and descriptions for the person. So, there's different ways to do it, but in terms of not violating the law—or in terms of not terminating somebody simply because they're thinking about starting a union—that typically wouldn't be in an employee handbook anyway.

If the law has one standard, and you set a higher standard in your employee handbook, then you're going to be held to your own higher standard. And if you don't know what that standard is because you've never read the handbook the person who pitched it to you crafted, and you don't know what the procedures are because they're not even really your procedures, you could create problems for yourself. Because if you don't follow that exact handbook to the letter, it's very easy for an employee to say they were discriminated against or weren't afforded the processes outlined in the handbook that they believed would be applied to all employees.

It is important to have solid procedures that you regularly follow on write-ups. But if your handbook describes a process of progressive discipline for employees, where you escalate the discipline depending on the circumstances, and you then terminate somebody without following that progressive discipline exactly as it is phrased, then it's a very easy lawsuit.

If you say you're going to do something, you're going to be held to it. If you make an exception to that rule because your gut tells you it's not going to be worthwhile, then you're just setting yourself up for that lawsuit.

I'm not saying there is no benefit to having an employee handbook. They can be beneficial as long as you strictly and accurately follow it and regularly update it. But if you're not going to do those things—if you're not committed to it—then you're better off without one.

Beware of the false sense of security an employee handbook can engender. It can make you feel you've got every situation covered. But your handbook is not going to have an exhaustive list of every single employment law that you've got to follow. Some laws are for such specific, nuanced situations that it won't seem necessary to include them. But those laws you leave out still apply to your business, so if you rely too much on the handbook, you might miss something.

Now, my firm does not have an employee handbook. But to be fair, I know this area of the law much better than most people, so I can make strategic, calculated decisions when I terminate and can see the angles ahead of time. But most people aren't running an employment law firm, so they don't necessarily have that familiarity with the rules and the laws. Which is why I think it's important to at least talk to your attorney or your HR professional regarding potential legal liability before terminating somebody, eliminating their position, or laying them off.

I'm mainly giving this advice to smaller companies. If you've got five to ten employees and create an employee handbook, but as the owner, you're still too busy to actually work through the handbook, completely understand it, and participate in drafting it, then you're inviting more liability for yourself than actually solving any problems. But if you have a hundred plus employees, it probably makes sense for you to have an employee handbook, because you want to make sure things are being doled out fairly, and that there's a specific process in place. So, it helps you think through the issue.

And look, maybe you have a business, and you just love procedure. You love being involved in this kind of thing and can commit to ensuring that this employee handbook is reviewed. You'll make sure everybody is trained on it and understands it. You will ensure it's regularly updated as the laws change, and you'll make sure your staff is aware of those changes so that everybody follows the employee handbook.

In that case, you may find an employee handbook very helpful.

Know Your Laws

You have to know what the employment laws are to follow them. And there can be federal, state, and local laws that affect you. For example, you've got a federal minimum wage, a state minimum wage, and you can also have a city or a county minimum wage. And you are obligated to pay whichever of those is higher. So, you can say, "Yes, I comply with state minimum law," but if you're not also complying with the city and county, then you're not actually in compliance with the law. That's why you've got to be hyper-specific—you might have requirements at a very specific jurisdictional level of your county or city.

That being said, there are some employment laws you will encounter in most places, either because they're federal law or because they are laws that most states have.

Unions

You cannot legally prevent, disrupt, or penalize employees for engaging in labor activities through labor unions. All you can really do is negotiate with them and keep a good relationship with them. If you hear that somebody's trying to form a labor union and terminate them, you can then have a potential claim from that person saying that you unlawfully terminated them for trying to form a union.

Termination

Generally, even in California, the rule is you are allowed to terminate at will, unless you have a specific employment agreement for a specific period of time. You can terminate anybody for any reason whatsoever, except for a prohibited reason, which as I've mentioned before includes pregnancy, race, religion, and other such things.

Now, sometimes you might think an employee is making up a medical condition, so you refuse to make accommodations, such as giving them time off for medical appointments, or you just summarily fire them because you think they're trying to pull one over on you. That's a very easy way to mess things up and invite a lawsuit. Your documentation is admissible in a court of law, but your suspicions are not.

So, in terms of compliance, it's not easy to properly terminate somebody, and if you haven't set things up the right way early enough, then you could be inviting a lawsuit later. It's like a game of chess. When chess masters lose a game, they can point to someplace many moves earlier where they actually lost.

When you haven't anticipated the moves early enough and well enough, you're setting yourself up for the inevitability of the checkmate and the loss of a lawsuit. That's what you want to prevent.

Harassment and Discrimination Issues

There's an old jest: "The joke was so funny that human resources wanted to hear it." It's a way of reminding you that you should never, ever tell a joke that gets the attention of human resources, even if (or especially if) you own the business.

Simple remarks or jokes that you believe are funny can be taken out of context, so make sure that you have a clear understanding of what can constitute harassment. Remember, as a business owner, you need to act like a business owner at all times. Even if you think of employees as your friends, don't cross that line between employer and employee. They are your employees, and you need to act accordingly, whether it's the middle of the day at the office or at an end-of-week company happy hour.

Remember that everything you say can and will be used against you—inappropriate jokes, inappropriate comments, and improper touching can all result in significant liability against you as an individual, and also against your business.

You need to be on your guard against any kind of off-color humor, or any statements or actions that suggest sexism, discrimination, or racism. You also need to monitor what communications are being sent out, because what you say on social media, in text messages, or in emails can and probably will be used against you later if issues such as harassment or discrimination come up.

A good rule of thumb for jokes is this: Don't criticize or make fun of any kind of immutable characteristic of a person or anything that's very specific or personal to that person, like their race, religion, accent, or sexual orientation. But if you want to make fun of somebody because of the sports team they follow, that's fine.

When it comes to sexual harassment, generally speaking, if you're making a comment to somebody that's sexual in nature and/or specifically about their sex or their sexual orientation, then it could be considered sexual harassment. And there is no excuse. You can't say things like, "It's not really improper, because I called him gay even though he's straight." That's still improper.

A lot of people don't get this, because wherever they grew up, this behavior may have been normal or common. And now all of a sudden, they're making jokes or saying things that were accepted where they were but are entirely inappropriate in the workplace.

Harassment training is mandatory in California for businesses of a certain size with a certain number of employees, so make sure they get it.

You also need to make sure the management at your office is properly trained to handle any situation that arises. If management hasn't been properly trained on what harassment is and how complaints regarding harassment or racial discrimination should be handled, it can result in huge liability against you and your company.

So, be careful about what you're sending, and be careful about what you're saying. This isn't a matter of being politically correct, this is a matter of making sure that you're protecting yourself and your business by stamping out the behaviors that most commonly lead to lawsuits.

Misclassification of Employees

The misclassification of employees as independent contractors is against federal law, but it's an especially huge liability here in California—because if you misclassify somebody, it has a snowball effect, getting bigger and bigger and bigger. Misclassifying someone as an independent contractor instead of an employee is also an easy thing to get wrong in California.

This is because California's Assembly Bill 5 set forth a three-part "ABC test" that you have to pass for somebody to be properly considered an independent contractor. Otherwise, that person is considered an employee. This is different from many other states, including how the IRS looks at it.

In California, if you have someone working for you, they can only be considered an independent contractor if a, b, and c are met: (a) they are free of your direction and control, (b) they are doing work that is not usually done as part of your business, and (c) they are in an independently established business that does the type of work they're doing for you.

For example, let's say you've got a marketing agency, and you need a logo design. Well, if your marketing agency designs logos from time to time, that's going to be considered a core part of your business. It means that you can't pay someone to design a logo for your company—or for one of your company's customers—and classify them as an independent contractor.

You have to be careful about this. Because when you don't pay somebody properly—meaning you pay them as an independent contractor instead of an employee—they've got all kinds of claims for damages: things like not giving them their meal and rest breaks, the required itemized wage statements, or appropriate overtime pay.

The way AB 5 is written, the claims of the "misclassified employee" are presumed to be true unless you have written records that show otherwise. So, if you've got somebody who says they were working five hours of overtime every day, then you can have additional penalties and be on the hook for their attorney's fees.

In terms of the overall damages, $1,000 can easily balloon up to $5,000 to $10,000 for every $1,000. If you've had a relationship with this individual that's gone on for a few months, or a year or more, that can come out to be a tremendous sum of money.

Now, not every state has a law as strict as AB 5. But wherever your business is, you absolutely need to know what the laws are around classifying employees as independent contractors.

In general, know the employment laws that apply in your area and follow them, or you could get into real trouble. If you're not sure, contact a lawyer to help you think through these issues. Keep in mind that it is cheaper to avoid issues than it is to resolve them after violations have occurred.

CHAPTER 8

When to Fight and When to Settle

When engaged in a legal battle, there is a time to fight and a time to settle. That decision can be difficult. And even if fighting makes sense at the beginning, when you're being sued or suing someone else, the prospects of a case can sometimes turn on a dime. If the case drags on and legal expenses grow, your fight may no longer be worth the cost.

There are a number of considerations in deciding whether fighting or settling is appropriate. When we sit down with clients who have a conflict to resolve, we want to make sure we understand their goals, their general budget, and their ideal outcome. Only then can we determine the best way to advise them on how to proceed.

There are any number of points at which a case can settle. It can get settled before a lawsuit is filed or after it's filed. It can also get settled right before, during, or even after the trial. The

THE ENTREPRENEUR'S LEGAL PLAYBOOK

optimal point for a settlement will vary from one case to the next, depending on variables and circumstances specific to that case. So, if you decide to fight, it doesn't mean you can't choose to settle later when the time is more favorable.

Is The Fight Worth It?

Paying a lawyer to fight your case is a business investment, and as with any business investment, you want to know what sort of return you're getting on it. You want to know if that investment will save or cost you in the long-term compared with settling.

But as with any investment, there is an unavoidable element of risk, and no result is ever guaranteed. For example, if you fight and lose, you could be worse off than if you settled. But there are also risks to a quick settlement.

That's why it's so important to have a thorough discussion with your lawyer—to advise you well, they need to understand your needs, budget, and the strengths and weaknesses of your case.

We had a client who was facing a million-dollar claim. The client didn't want to pay over a million dollars, so they came to us for an assessment. We looked at the case and thought the case wasn't worth more than one hundred thousand. So, fighting the claim seemed well worth it. We litigated the case and resolved it for about seventy-five thousand dollars. That, plus attorney's fees of fifty thousand meant the client laid out about $125,000 instead of a million. That's a solid return on investment.

When a case is far more expensive to settle than it's going to cost you in attorney's fees, a good rule of thumb is to find a good attorney to fight it.

But what if the cost of litigation is greater than the cost of settling? If someone is suing you for fifty thousand dollars, they have a strong claim, and the litigation costs are likely to be another fifty thousand—so it might make more sense to settle.

Fighting to Send a Message

There are times, though, when you might consider fighting even if it might cost you more in the short-term than a quick settlement would.

I had a client facing a demand for a complete refund from two people who claimed my client hadn't performed on a certain agreement. This was a little over one hundred thousand dollars. However, there were clear indications that my client had performed many of the tasks required. The disagreement was simply whether everything was performed in accordance with the contract. The other side argued that it hadn't been.

My client was taking a risk by going all the way through the trial process in this case. There's always a risk that you can lose. But there's also the risk that even if you do win, the other side might not be able to pay anything they owe you.

But my client took on those risks, because he wanted to make a point that he was not an easy target for a shakedown. For him, the value of the case went beyond this one-time situation. It was a way to send a message to any others who might be looking to come after him.

Ultimately, we won—and because the contract they had contained a prevailing party attorney's fees and costs clause, the other side owed my client damages, plus costs and attorney's fees, which we recovered for him.

Making a quick settlement on a frivolous case could make you look like an easy target who will settle all of their cases to avoid litigation. That can open the floodgates for other potential plaintiffs against your business. Sometimes there is value in sending the message that you are not to be trifled with.

Now, if you have a tiny business, there are few people to send a message to, and nobody's really going to hear that message anyway. So, for a small business, it may not make financial sense to spend a lot of money trying to send a message intended for a broader audience than the one you have.

But sometimes, people will want to send a message for a narrow audience. For example, I'm representing a business owner whose business is not that big. But he got a demand from an ex-employee who was terminated for certain reasons involving a misclassification issue.

They could try and send the message to that employee. But the reality of the case was that there were technical legal violations that could escalate and cause a lot more damage. Instead of sending a message of "Don't even try and sue us," you can wind up just sending a message that you have problems other people might be able to exploit.

In that situation, trying to send a message would be like trying to put out a grease fire with water—you're going to spread it everywhere. You have to understand what kind of fire you've got. If it's a trash fire, dump some water on it. If you've got an oil fire in your kitchen, pouring water on it could burn down your house.

You have to understand your situation and do what makes most sense for that scenario. There is no cookie-cutter approach. Not every lawsuit should be fought, but not every lawsuit should be settled either. It just depends on the specific circumstances—what the best- and worst-case scenarios are. Once you understand that, you can make a strategic, calculated decision rather than an emotional one. When I recommend fighting to send a message, it's never an emotional "how dare they." It's only when sending a message makes strategic and financial sense.

Sometimes, even when a lawsuit is blatantly frivolous or unjustified, it actually makes greater financial sense to swallow the cost and move on, no matter how infuriating that may be.

When Fighting Stops Making Sense

Sometimes a case that looks like a good bet can get shaky, and you'll have to reevaluate.

For example, a few years ago I represented a cosmetics manufacturer. One of their customers, who was a retail seller, had a little over $500,000 in invoices they just hadn't paid. And then, all of a sudden, when faced with the bill, the retail seller claimed the cosmetics were faulty and problematic. They said they didn't pay because they were getting a bunch of returns of the cosmetics manufactured by my client, and they had switched to a different manufacturer.

The case ended up in litigation, and when I deposed the person at that company who was most knowledgeable about those returns and claims, I was able to poke big holes in their case. While the company claimed that they had more returns for my client's goods than for their other manufacturers, I got him to admit that all the returned goods looked the same, were destroyed upon return, and that the company did not track who had manufactured those returned goods. So, they had no actual way to know which of my client's goods were actually being returned.

I glanced over at opposing counsel and saw he was squirming, because this fact destroyed their whole theory of the case.

At that point, the tide was turning in our favor. But tides go both ways. The next thing we knew, a witness came out of the blue— an ex-employee of my client who'd been terminated. She came in as a "star witness," willing to testify to all of these things that supposedly happened at my client's shop, and how she was told to do all of these improper things.

My client said that the ex-employee made it all up. But she was making all these claims under the penalty of perjury, so it looked bad for my client. And I hadn't been told about this employee until she came out of the woodwork, so I had no way to plan for her testimony ahead of time.

This put us in a precarious situation. First, there was a very real possibility that her testimony could cause our complaint to be seen as not credible, and we would lose the case. But even worse, the millions of dollars of business my client and her company had previously done together would now be an issue, because this lady was an employee during that whole period.

So that is a case where it suddenly made more sense to just settle for a mutual walk-away, where we dropped our suit and the other side dropped theirs. The risks of continuing had just gotten too high.

Things to Consider Before You Fight

There are a number of things to consider when deciding whether or not to fight. It all depends on the circumstances of the case, but here are some things you'll want to think about in the beginning.

What's Your Budget?

Your budget is like a war chest—the bigger it is, the more you can spend to try and win the fight. You need to have some idea of how much you can afford to spend on fighting a claim.

What's Their Budget?

A big budget is relative, and if the fight is with someone who has a huge financial advantage, that has to be taken into consideration. Just because the other side has a huge budget doesn't mean it's unlimited.

There are reasons for companies to settle even if they have the ability to outspend you and wear you down. For example, a public company may not want certain information to come out, or for a particular kind of lawsuit to be listed in a quarterly or yearly risk report. Sometimes they would rather settle than disclose their risk. They may want to settle by the end of the year just to clear it out of the way.

But it is possible to budget so much to a case that you can simply exhaust the other side. If the other side has a budget that's ten times the size of yours, you just have to factor that into your calculations.

How Long Are You Willing to Keep Going?

The quicker you settle a case, the quicker it's done and you can move on. But it can cost you a lot to speed things up. So, you need to decide how much of a hurry you're in and how much you'll pay for a faster resolution.

The quickest approach might be to just pay whatever it takes to settle a case, but this might wind up costing you more time in additional lawsuits later on if you develop a reputation as a chronic settler.

Are You Up for a Fight?

Litigation is a taxing and stressful emotional rollercoaster. So, you want to make sure you're mentally and emotionally prepared to deal with the ups and downs. Sometimes during litigation, it will look like things aren't going your way. You lose on a motion or a negotiation point. This can be very upsetting. Then, all of a sudden, you can find yourself winning every point and thinking you're on a glide path to success. And then, you can hit another obstacle.

I tell clients that these moments are just battles in a war. Losing some battles doesn't mean you're going to lose the war, and sometimes you have to pick the battles that are the ones most worth fighting.

It's a lot for some people, so you need to decide if you're up for it.

Do You Have the Time?

You've got a business to run, so you have to consider how much time you can give to a lawsuit. The right attorney and law firm should be able to handle most of the litigation for you without needing much input from you. But when it comes to things like discovery, you will have to verify discovery responses, which means stating that they're true and correct under penalty of perjury. But a good attorney and law firm will make that as seamless as possible, so it doesn't suck up too much of your time.

Understanding Costs

When considering fighting a lawsuit, you need to understand what costs you'll wind up paying regardless of whether you win or lose.

In some countries, like Britain, whoever loses a lawsuit pays for both side's legal costs and lawyer fees. But in America, generally speaking, each side bears its own costs. You'll have to pay things like filing fees, deposition costs, and your attorney's fees and expenses. You don't get any of that back if you win the case.

There are two exceptions to this rule:

1) By contract: It is possible to include a prevailing attorney's fee provision in your contracts stipulating that, in the event of a legal dispute, the winner can recoup its attorney's fees from the loser. If that provision is in a contract between the conflicted parties, the court or the arbitrator is supposed to award attorney's fees to the winner. This is true as long as you follow the procedure set out in your agreement, as well as whatever procedures are required by the arbitration venue or court you're in.

You might wonder if you can write a contract where you get your attorney's fees if you win, but you don't have to pay anyone's legal fees if you lose. It's a clever idea, but at least in California it's not possible. No matter how you phrase that provision, it will be interpreted in California's courts as applying to both sides. I don't want to speak to the rest of the U.S., but in California, this is not going to work for you.

You may not always want to include an attorney's fees provision in your contract. If it's a contract with a small business that wouldn't ever have the money to pay those fees, and you're a bigger company with more assets, then all you've done is create a contract that will force you to pay their attorney's fees if they win but probably won't get you a dime if you lose. So, make sure you think about that before you sign a contract that could backfire on you.

2) By statute: There are certain statutes, both federal and state, that can allow you to recoup attorney's fees if you win. However, these are typically consumer-facing statutes designed to protect individuals or consumers rather than business owners.

For example, in California, employees can recoup attorney's fees if they have been wrongfully terminated, weren't paid for all their hours, or didn't get all of their meal and rest breaks. In that case, the individual can recover attorney's fees if they win, while the employer generally can't get their attorney's fees back if they lose. This is something to be aware of if you're ever involved in an employment lawsuit.

But in a business against business cases, it's rare for these statutes to apply to either party. There are certain exceptions, including in copyright or trademark infringement claims, but these are rare.

So, if you want your attorney's fees covered when you win a lawsuit, make sure that you have it stipulated in your contracts with all your vendors or customers.

A Tough Decision

As you can see, there is a lot to think about when faced with the choice of fighting or settling. The important thing is to make that decision with the advice of good legal counsel that can walk you through these considerations and help you come to a decision that makes sense.

CHAPTER 9

Managing a Crisis

For a family business, a legal crisis like a big lawsuit creates strong emotions. Because it's not just a business. It's not just your livelihood. It's your legacy. You'll say, "I built a business for my children and their children someday; I worked tirelessly to pass something along to them. And now, people have come and threatened to take that all away."

I saw this with a client who built a family carpeting business with his sons in California.

The way he ran his business, he treated the professional carpet installers he worked with as contractors, paying by the job—for years.

Then he was hit with a Private Attorney General Act ("PAGA") lawsuit saying his employees were improperly classified as independent contractors and weren't properly paid for all their time. The lawsuit demanded $1.8 million. PAGA cases are notoriously difficult on employers because not only are the laws that result in PAGA claims strict, but plaintiffs' attorneys get their fees paid by the employer under the law.

PAGA incentivizes private attorneys to bring lawsuits on behalf of aggrieved employees who, for example, didn't get their meal breaks or weren't paid overtime. It's a way for the state to enforce employment laws and get a cut of any settlement without having to do the legal work themselves. So, there are lawyers who search for these cases. If they find employees who qualify, the resulting claim will be split between the state, the lawyers, and the employees. And the lawyer can attach additional employees to the claim.

PAGA cases can be hard on the employer, who must pay the employees' attorneys' fees if they lose but can't recoup their own attorneys' fees if they win. So, as you fight your case, your own legal costs go up as the other side's—that you may eventually have to pay—also go up. This means the other side doesn't have a huge incentive to resolve the case, because they know that you're going to be on the hook no matter what.

Employers will almost certainly have to pay all those costs, because there is almost never a good faith defense. The rules are pretty black-and-white, so if you've committed violations, you're not getting out of it.

PAGA cases will also result in penalties paid to the state. In California, labor law violations go through the individual owners of the company, so you are personally on the hook.

In a crisis like this, it is important to have two things: the right people and the right mindset.

Creating the Right Team

My law firm was not the first legal representation hired by the carpeting business. They had hired a lawyer they felt some cultural connection with, but he had not moved the case forward. In fact, things were getting worse. So, they reached out to another lawyer. That lawyer, who only worked with cases like this on the other side, referred them to us—because they knew that we do a great job on the defense side.

It's important to make sure the people you have on your team have experience, know what they're doing, and get good results with cases like yours. Business owners are sometimes tempted to hire someone because they have a personal connection, or someone from the same ethnic group as themselves, but if they don't have the necessary track record, then that can be a huge mistake. Not every lawyer is suited to handle every kind of case.

Ultimately, it comes down to having counsel that understands you, understands your business, and can create goals and strategies based on that understanding instead of using a cookie-cutter strategy approach that could end up costing a lot of time, money and headaches.

It's also important that you work well with your legal representation. As with any crisis, it helps to:

- Have clear expectations and goals,

- Maintain clear communication with your legal counsel and the rest of your team,

- Make sure that your documents and information are well-organized so you can navigate all of these complex issues successfully.

Having the Right Mindset

Mindset is so critical when it comes to success. It's also critical when dealing with a crisis, where you need to keep your emotional equilibrium and stay grounded.

One typical reaction that my clients have when they're being sued is to want to shrink down and slow down business. Many times, they should be doing the exact opposite. Instead of shrinking down, they should be looking for ways to expand, ways to do more business, and ways to get more clients.

Expansion is critical because any lawsuit is going to require capital. It will take money to fund the lawsuit. Not only are there the attorney's fees and costs, but there's a need to have money set aside in case you need to pay for a settlement. Even if you're just looking to resolve it as soon as possible, you're still going to need capital to be able to do that. The more capital you can pull in, the better off you're going to be. That's why you should continue to scale and grow your business while you're involved in a lawsuit.

Of course, this advice does not apply if your growth and expansion is related to what you're getting sued for. If someone has filed a lawsuit accusing you of unlawful marketing or unlawful sales, and you really have been doing unlawful marketing or unlawful sales, then you should not continue your growth by continuing to violate the law. But if you're doing everything legally and ethically, then you want to keep looking for ways to grow and scale your business. That's your best bet for getting to a favorable resolution of your case.

One worry clients have when they're hit by a lawsuit is that if they keep getting bigger, they are going to attract more legal attacks.

Are the problems just going to continue to grow if I continue to scale? If I have this one problem now that I'm at three million dollars in revenue, will I have ten times the lawsuits and headaches at thirty million? While it's not that linear, a bigger company probably will be hit by more lawsuits. So, it's important to have the mindset that you're going to be able to weather the storm.

A future of dealing with more lawsuits seems terrifying when you're working through your first legal crisis, but the truth is, it's part of owning a thriving business. You will have lawyers to handle the heavy lifting in a lawsuit while you keep your focus and energy on the things that help you and the things that will help your business survive so you can go through litigation and come out on the other side.

Dealing with lawsuits is like riding a bike. In the beginning, when you're first learning, you're going to fall a number of times. Then you get your balance and learn how to maneuver the bike. It doesn't mean you're never going to fall. It just means you're more prepared to handle the bike. Even if you lose control, you're still less likely to fall than in the very beginning, because you're just getting a feel for it.

You don't know what you don't know, and eventually, the learning curve of figuring out what you don't know flattens out.

Avoid the "Why me?" mindset. Owners think they will be the one company that doesn't get sued because they did everything right. They feel they've been singled out and attacked for this thing that seemingly everybody else does. Somehow, they're the one business that got caught and is getting sued. Meanwhile, Jack up the street is doing the same thing, and he's doing fine.

But the reality is, most businesses end up facing their first lawsuit somewhere between one million and ten million in revenue, because it's at that point that they have a real business. They've interacted with enough people or companies, whether it's internally or externally, that somebody's going to have some kind of issue or problem. This is what comes with the territory, and this is why a lot of people don't make it in business. You just have to accept and expect that this is par for the course. And so, the best thing you can do is just be prepared for it, mentally, financially, and strategically.

Keeping Your Equilibrium

It can be hard to keep your emotions in check during a crisis. You may feel you just can't deal with all the stress. So, you need to find something that helps you manage your emotions and the stress that comes with a crisis, which will be different for everyone.

For some people, therapy will help, while others think therapy is a complete waste of time. Some people find exercise and meditation helpful, while others feel that it stresses them out more.

One great approach when dealing with that pressure and stress is to focus on what you can control and what you can do. What changes can you make now into the future to keep this from happening again? What procedures do you need to put into place? How do you continue growing your business, but in the right ethical and legal way, because this is a problem that you still have to deal with? Of course, in business, there's always some aspect of reactivity—but if you can plan ahead, you're more likely to come out ahead.

Weathering a Lawsuit

A lawsuit can put a big strain on you and your business. You want to minimize how much a legal crisis affects your ability to do business, because as I keep saying, you want to keep growing your business even when in the midst of a legal crisis.

Don't Get Caught Up in the Day-to-Day

If you're running a business, you don't want to spend any more time than you have to on the case you're fighting. While your lawyers are handling your legal strategy, someone still has to communicate with the lawyers—but that doesn't always have to be you. You have internal legal counsel who doesn't have expertise in litigation but is still certainly able to deal with outside counsel. If you have an assistant, you can have them talk to the lawyers and keep you apprised of what's happening.

There will still be high-level meetings you'll want to be a part of, but ideally, you will have as little day-to-day involvement as possible, because that will just waste time you could be spending scaling your business.

What if You Don't Have Enough Money?

Fighting a lawsuit isn't cheap, so if you aren't pulling enough money every month to cover your legal costs, you will need to find that money.

One option is litigation funding. There are companies that will loan you money specifically to keep you afloat if legal costs are overwhelming you. Litigation funding is high risk and high reward for the company offering it, so it's not cheap, but it's there if you need it.

It's good to explore all the ways you can support your lawsuit. Some people are able to borrow money from their friends or family. Some businesses have even set up GoFundMe campaigns, which can work if your customers really, really love you.

Sometimes there are government grants and programs for certain populations, like minority-owned businesses. While I don't know of any specific grants or programs that fund litigation, it's worth researching what's out there that could help you in other ways.

If you get an offer for a credit card with 0 percent interest for the first year, that can be a good option as long as you have a plan to pay that money before the year is up and the interest rate increases.

Recovery: When the Dust Settles

Sooner or later, your lawsuit will settle. In the case of our client who had the PAGA lawsuit, we did pretty well. The average settlement for a PAGA claim is $1.1 million, but with some maneuvering, we managed to get it resolved for my client paying $125,000. That is still a lot of money, but it's a remarkable settlement given the clear violations, and it was low enough that the business didn't go under.

Keep in mind that no law firm, including ours, can guarantee you will come out of a lawsuit with so little financial harm. But if you can survive a lawsuit, you can continue to scale up your business so that when the next claim against you comes, you are in a far better position, financially and emotionally, to deal with it.

One thing you will want to do is minimize the openings for future claims. You want to make sure you are doing everything legally. Originally, we focused only on litigation and did not work with companies on restructuring their operations to discourage lawsuits. Eventually I realized that if I really wanted to make the kind of difference that I wanted to make, we should be offering those types of prevention services. From our litigation work, I know exactly how companies get attacked, how depositions go, how trials can go, and what evidence opposing lawyers are looking for. So now, we use our knowledge gained through litigation to help clients on the compliance side.

A Good Outcome

I want to tell you a story about a crisis that turned into an opportunity. It's not about a business dealing with employment violations. It's not even about defending a business in a lawsuit. It's a different kind of case altogether. But it's a good example of not only moving on from a crisis but of using it as an opportunity.

Years ago, a newlywed—let's call him Frank—bought a home from a house flipper, which is someone who buys a house, fixes it, and then sells it for profit.

Frank and his wife, we'll call her Patricia, went on a honeymoon to Australia, where Patrica was from. When they returned, they finally entered their new home, and it was a disaster. It was nothing like what he had bought. There was mold everywhere. The walls were soaked and bubbly. Roaches and insects had gotten into the house. It was not fit to live in. So, he came to me to ask me to help him fix it.

This case, like every case, had challenges. We were dealing with an experienced flipper who had bought and sold the house through an LLC. The message was clear: "We're never going to pay you." His attorney said the LLC had no money—it had already been distributed—and blamed my clients for not doing proper due diligence on the house before they bought it.

So, we got them into arbitration, and we settled the case for a little over half the selling price, which was hundreds of thousands of dollars.

It was enough money that, after Frank got the house fixed, he had money left over. He thought: "That house flipper did everything so badly, but I could do this business the right way." So, he took some of the extra money, bought a duplex, and then went into the real estate business, because he saw what had been done wrong. He has since made himself successful in that business and currently owns several properties throughout Los Angeles.

Ultimately, Frank did well for himself. However, it started as complete devastation, and he didn't know what to do at first. This house was his largest purchase ever; he'd just gotten married, and now they were homeless, sleeping in his wife's photography studio and dealing with the strains of this huge crisis in their new marriage. But after we got the case resolved for him, he was able to take that misfortune and turn it into an opportunity for himself and his wife. He did exactly what I say clients should do, which is to just focus on your future, focus on how you put it together, and how you can come out of this thing.

I think that with every disaster or problem comes a greater opportunity. You just have to find it. Sometimes it's harder to find than others, but if you look hard enough and long enough, you'll find it.

CHAPTER 10

Lawsuit Preparation

The key to winning in anything is preparation. There are certain things you can do at the beginning of a lawsuit, like organizing documents, that will help your case. There are things you should be doing throughout business that will put you in a better position if you are in a legal entanglement.

A Well-Documented Case

Well-organized, comprehensive documents can be tremendously effective.

For example, I had a client who had been hired to create a prototype device for a company that was trying to get their product concept on *Shark Tank*, a TV series that connects entrepreneurs with investors. The company sued my client, saying that the prototype had not worked as it was supposed to, and they were entitled to a refund. My client agreed that his first prototype had some bugs, which is typical of prototypes, but said that he had fixed the bugs, so it worked properly, thus completing the work as agreed.

When I took him on as a client, I explained how important it would be for me to have any documents that would support his version of events: emails, copies of agreements, text messages, and the like. The good news was he had all of that, and he brought everything to me, perfectly organized.

Organizing Documents

When we have a new client, we'll ask them to organize their documents electronically, or they can pay us to do that for them. We start by organizing everything into folders such as agreements, emails, and text messages. We then internally name and organize the documents using the naming format, "yyyy. mm.dd-description of doc." So, you could have a document titled "2019.04.17-contract.doc." This lets you sort files chronologically with a simple name sort. With this method, you can quickly find any documents from the same time period. If you have an email, for example, you can see what texts were sent before and after that email.

As you can imagine, setting this up is tedious and time-consuming, but it helps tremendously when putting together your arguments and gaining a better understanding of what happened and when. It's much more helpful than relying on human memory, which fades. When you're talking about something that happened a few years ago, you're not going to remember all the context of the emails, text messages, etc., and so saved communications can help you refresh your own memory about what transpired or what was going on at that time when something happened.

Ideally, documents should be digitized, because otherwise you could be dealing with boxes and boxes full of paper that have to be manually sorted. It is extremely time-consuming, and therefore extremely expensive, to go through those.

We have a high-density scanner for digitizing documents that scans hundreds of pages every few minutes. They don't have to take up much room—some high-density scanners fit on a tabletop. Once digitized, you can use optical character recognition to search through documents, which is a much easier way to find certain phrases. Even AI could potentially sort your documents for you.

In an increasingly modernized world, your edge is efficiency and speed. So, the more quickly and efficiently you can do something compared with your opposition, the more of an advantage you're going to have. The faster your attorney can find the information they are looking for—the faster they can use it—the faster they can move your case forward.

This is also very important in trials. You might have thousands of pages to work with, so it's important to be able to quickly find a specific line. This is especially true when you've got somebody on the witness stand who says something, and you're trying to remember exactly where something was in ten thousand pages of documents. If you've got digitized documents, you've got the best of both worlds—you can quickly flip to something on paper, or you can do a quick search through your computer for what you need.

Electronic copies also make it much easier to back things up, which has become extra important as we've seen more and more floods and fires in certain parts of the country. When we've handled claims against insurance companies for failing to pay, the first question they always ask is, "What documentation do you have?" Then when you say, "Oh, well, you know the documentation was damaged or destroyed in the fire and/or the flood," they're not as understanding as you'd want them to be. They usually use that as yet another reason to deny your claim.

So, you want to give yourself the best chance possible to have a winning case. The easiest way to do that is to stay organized from the beginning, rather than trying to pull it all together at the end.

Documentation Strengthens Your Case

Among my client's well-organized documentation, we found an email that became a critical key to winning that case. And it's a good example of how important it is to use—and keep—written communication with those you work with.

So many details come up during the course of a project after the contract has been signed. If someone says, "add this feature" or "make it less red" or "make it 20 percent bigger," you want that documented. When you say, "He and I talked about it, and we agreed to this," and the other side says, "No, that's not the conversation we had," a lack of documentation puts you in a bad position. A judge, jury or arbitrator will find documents and written things far more credible than what you claim you remember about something that happened months or years ago.

Written communication gives you a record of day-to-day interactions and lessens the danger of simply forgetting important details. If you have a conversation, it is wise to send an email confirming what you said in that discussion to the other side. That way, later you can say, "Look, not only did we talk about it, but I sent that person a confirming email, and here it is. They didn't reply to it, or they didn't disagree with it, which they certainly would have if it had been incorrect."

Obviously, the more detail you've got in these communications, the better off you'll be in a lawsuit. But as with all things, there's balance. You may not need to give a five-page recap email for a ten-minute conversation, but you want to communicate the main points that were discussed and what was agreed on. A good guideline is to state who does what by what date. The more specific you make that, the easier it is to prove things later.

Documentation Optics

Documenting discussions and agreements while doing business is important in case of a lawsuit, but as you're documenting interactions, you need to consider how what you say would sound to those judging your case if you had to go to court.

That's why it's important to keep communications professional. Avoid derogatory language or curse words in written and verbal communications, even when emotions are running high. Treat each email or text message as if it might be read in front of a judge or jury one day. If you think it would be embarrassing to have it read out loud, or if you think it would put you in a bad light, then don't write it that way.

There is no case in which a jury or arbitrator is going to say, "He just said this curse word because he's fired up. He couldn't help using this language because he was so wronged, so obviously he should win." That doesn't happen.

How An Unanswered Email Helped Win a Case

My client had kept all their communication on the prototype project with the company, and one email I found in the back-and-forth over the project became really critical. It was the email where my client said something like, "I have fixed the prototype and tested it. It now works properly, when do you want to pick it up?"

And their reply was...nothing. They never replied to that email at all.

So, in arbitration, I said, "He sent you this email that I have not seen a reply to. Did you send a reply?"

"Oh, I'm sure we did."

"So, where is that email? Because you were supposed to produce all the emails, but you don't have it in your binders, and we certainly don't have it in ours. If there was a reply, where did it go?"

You might wonder why someone would have a prototype created and then ghost the contractor. Our whole theory of the case was that they had tried to get this product idea onto *Shark Tank*, and when *Shark Tank* passed, they had abandoned the project and simply wanted to get back the money they'd spent on it.

In arbitration, they were forced to turn over emails with *Shark Tank* in which they were specifically told the project wasn't a fit, but that they could reach out in the future.

But on cross-examination, they admitted that they had never reached out to *Shark Tank* again, had never picked up the prototype, and had never even responded to the email.

The biggest thing was, they could not get around the fact that they never picked up the working prototype. We had video of my client testing it that showed it did, in fact, work. The company had argued that there was further work my client hadn't completed, and that they should get their money back for that. But he had been unable to complete that further work because they had never picked up the prototype, thus preventing him from moving forward.

The arbitrator agreed with our contentions, and one of the things that persuaded him to side with us was that email.

I'm not saying that our client would have lost without that email—we had other strong points in the case, but I like to reduce variability as much as possible, and that email significantly reduced variability.

On a related note, judges, arbitrators, and juries tend to believe what they see much more than what they hear, so written evidence like emails, contracts, letters, and the like are extremely helpful when it comes to litigation and winning a case.

The Handshake Agreement Guy

Now, I'll tell you about a case from early in my career with a client who had almost no documentation at all, because he relied almost entirely on handshake deals and verbal conversations.

My client had purchased a store and alleged that the success of this store had been fraudulently misrepresented, with net income and revenue that was vastly less than what they had told him.

He had been told that the books were incorrect, showing an amount of revenue which was much lower than their net income claim, because they were taking the cash payments that they received from sales and not reporting them on their books or on the taxes. So, they claimed that the store was far more profitable than the books showed. They even let my client come in and sit in at the store for a few weeks to see what kind of revenue it was generating.

This is what my client told me, and I believed him. But it's not about what you know; it's about what you can prove.

In spite of what I would consider some red flags, my client purchased the store, paying a big chunk of the purchase price in cash. The other side claimed he hadn't paid it all, and while I had no doubt that my client did pay it, there wasn't anything like a formal receipt.

When my client realized the store was far less profitable than he'd been led to believe, he sued. And of course, the other side said, "Where's the documentation? Your guy came in, he looked at the books, and now he's saying that we were committing tax fraud, but he still wanted to go ahead with this purchase. He claims that he didn't really know what the net income was, even though he came in and sat at the store for weeks."

There wasn't much of a paper trail—the deal was put together through phone calls and in-person visits. That made it crazy difficult to be able to get the case resolved.

We did actually get a favorable resolution, but it took a lot of time. The case settled very close to trial, because they wanted to see if my client would just give up before then. We had to push it to the brink of trial to get them to agree to pay up, and we still only got them to pay half of what the case would have been worth with the proper documentation.

With little documentation to work with, I had to spend a lot of time talking to a number of people to try and piece things together, with each person describing events somewhat differently. If my client had had emails, receipts, texts, and a well-drafted contract, the case would likely have been settled much sooner with much less cost.

The Pros and Cons of Countersuits

The key to winning cases is leverage—how much leverage do you have, and what is it? When somebody sues you, that puts you on the defensive. One way to gain leverage is to go on offense with a strategic countersuit.

When considering a countersuit, you have to think about what kinds of claims you could make, which requires some analysis and a good lawyer to help you make that decision. You also need to look at whether you can afford it. A countersuit is not just a quick onslaught—you have to be able to maintain it. And if you can only budget enough to focus on defense or offense, you have to choose defense.

It's also important to consider how viable the claims of your countersuit would be. Although clients with bigger budgets often care less about the viability of the claims since even a frivolous countersuit will cost the other side time and money.

One thing that can change the calculation is if you have a contract with what's called a "prevailing party attorney's fees provision," which requires the loser to pay the other side's attorney's fees. Huge players will often try to run over small players by increasing their legal costs. They use the money they haven't paid you to out-litigate and outspend you until you give up. Many times, they come out ahead—if they owe you a million bucks, and spending three hundred grand in attorney's fees will force you to give up, they'll save seven hundred grand.

This is where that prevailing party attorney's fees provision comes in. If you have a contract with a company with deep pockets that contains such a provision, then the other side can play all the games they like but know that if they lose, they'll be out all the money they were forcing you to spend on lawyers.

That's what happened in the prototype case. The other side ended up paying my client's attorney's fees on top of what they had to pay my client because they lost their suit. It was, frankly, a dumb strategy. They spent multiples of what they owed my client to try to avoid paying my client.

One thing a prevailing party attorney's fees provision does is get both sides to more critically consider their position, because they could have to pay not only their own attorney's fees, but also the other side's attorney's fees.

We considered filing a countersuit against the company for failing to pay our client but chose not to because the prevailing party attorney's fees provision could have caused issues in getting those attorney's fees paid if there were a split decision.

When considering a countersuit, you have to consider the risk versus the reward. Do we have asymmetric risk? Is the reward much greater than the risk? If the risk is higher than the reward, or if the risk and reward are even, it isn't a good strategy unless there is some secondary advantage. For example, sometimes filing a countersuit can not only create leverage in your lawsuit, but it can also put your business in a better position to expand its position in the marketplace if it wins the countersuit. But in this case, there wasn't a secondary advantage.

If the other side had made a proper risk/reward analysis, they would not have taken this approach—it's something we pointed out to them numerous times. But they were so certain they were going to win that they were willing to spend anything. They paid one hundred thousand dollars for an expert witness with strong academic credentials, hoping to steamroll us on expertise. But the arbitrator found our witness, who didn't have a college degree but had a lot of practical experience in successfully designing and launching the types of products that were at issue in the case, more persuasive.

There are other cases where we almost always file countersuits, like partnership disputes. In those cases, there's almost always something that the other side did wrong, so we go on the counter-offensive.

It always depends on the specific case and the specific circumstances, but certain lawsuits lend themselves to countersuits and to counter-claims more than others.

Final Advice

Entrepreneurs are very optimistic by nature. But that optimism means they don't always think about what will happen if things go wrong, and how to prepare for that ahead of time. Optimism is good, but blind optimism can get you in trouble if you're not preparing for negative outcomes.

The best tip I can give when it comes to being prepared for lawsuits is to start with the end in mind. Ask yourself early on: What happens if this doesn't work? What if this person or company doesn't do what they said that they were going to do? How will I deal with that?

Ultimately, lawsuit preparation begins long before there's any hint you will be sued. It involves keeping your documents organized and documenting every important interaction. It involves staying professional. It involves having a clear, well-written agreement that puts the odds in your favor if something goes wrong.

If everything goes well and there are no problems, then you've spent a little extra time sending emails that you may never need. But if things go wrong, you will already be ahead of the game.

CHAPTER 11

How Do I Know I Have the Right Lawyer for Me?

Unfortunately, just because someone is a lawyer doesn't mean they are the right lawyer for you or your matter. I have had numerous clients come to my law firm asking me to help clean up the messes made by their previous lawyers.

For example, back when I was still in law school, my client Roberta had a lawyer helping her with a partnership dispute. When she came to me, it was about new claims related to that same partnership dispute that had started years before, when her partner had previously sued her.

Unfortunately, during the prior lawsuit, her lawyer had not filed a cross-complaint. That is, Roberta had been sued but hadn't filed a countersuit. That was a big concern, because it meant that the statute of limitations had run out on some of her claims.

The statute of limitations is like a game clock that starts ticking downwards when a lawsuit begins. Once it ticks down to zero, you can no longer successfully bring that claim forward.

In the first lawsuit, Roberta had claims she could have filed, and she wanted those claims brought. But her lawyer had never filed a cross-complaint. Her lawyer never even gave her the full file. I had to issue a subpoena and threaten to file a lawsuit against *him*, before he finally turned over the complete file so I could help my client.

That lawyer had not been very responsive to her, and he didn't give her detailed explanations of what he was doing or why. But she'd given him the benefit of the doubt, because he was a senior lawyer with decades of experience and a good pedigree.

By the time I had graduated from law school and passed the bar, her dispute had spanned well over eight years. That's when she hired me to represent her as a client. This current lawsuit had some overlap with a prior one. Unfortunately, that meant that the statute of limitations on certain claims she wanted to bring had run out because the former lawyer hadn't brought them.

In the first case, she had been sued by her partner. As the case got close to trial, that partner thought Roberta was likely to win, so he dismissed his lawsuit. Since she didn't have a cross-complaint, the end of the lawsuit left her unable to clarify her rights and responsibilities.

In the case I handled, she was suing her partner. Our argument was that this was a new claim with new facts, in which case the statute of limitations for her claims would not apply. But as I had warned her could happen, the judge saw it as essentially the same dispute from years ago. While the facts were new, they were based on the same essential core argument about ownership and ownership rights, and whether she genuinely had any ownership in this business. Therefore, the judge determined that she would have needed to have brought the claim forward in that prior lawsuit.

How People Wind Up with the Wrong Lawyer

When people wind up with a lawyer that doesn't work out for them, it's often because they didn't dig deep enough. They chose someone entirely because of a friend's recommendation, or a personal connection, or a similar cultural background, or impressive credentials, and they prioritized that over really digging into the lawyer's experience and results.

Roberta had trusted her lawyer's lengthy resume and prestigious law school experience, but that alone wasn't enough to get her the lawyer she actually needed.

What to Look for in a Lawyer

The key things to ask yourself when selecting a good lawyer are:

1. Have they handled similar cases?

2. What kind of results have they had?

3. Do they communicate clearly with you?

4. Do you feel comfortable with how they conduct themselves and explain things?

5. Are they responsive to your inquiries? Remember, if they are not responsive from the outset, they are likely not to be communicative later.

Experience, Knowledge, and Results

When choosing a lawyer, you can certainly look at whether they went to a good law school and have worked for impressive law firms. But even if they are knowledgeable about the law, law is a big subject, and not every lawyer is right for every case. You want the right lawyer for your specific situation. You want to hire someone who has handled similar cases.

Have They Handled Cases Like Yours?

You want a lawyer who has been successful—ideally in cases like yours. Ask them what cases they've had that are similar to yours, and ask about their results. Ask them how they've approached previous cases, and why those cases turned out the way they did. Ask for the case numbers of their previous cases so you can do your own research, and for prior clients who will give references. See if their website includes written or video testimonials from real clients. Check out their online reviews. Do not be shy about this or concerned about offending the person you are hiring.

Hiring the right lawyer is usually critical to winning your case, as well as to your peace of mind throughout the process.

Google the lawyer. A lot of things will come up in terms of whether they've ever personally been sued before, or whether they've had any disciplinary proceedings against them by the state bar.

In California, and I imagine in most states, you can also go to the state bar's website and search their name to see if they have any prior discipline against them. You can also find out things like when they were admitted to the state bar, where they went to undergrad, and where they went to law school. You should also take a look at the reviews to see what peers and clients say about this lawyer.

Do They Understand Business?

You want a lawyer who understands the challenges of running a business. Do they understand, for example, that if your business is seasonal, your ability to deal with legal matters may vary according to the time of year?

Ask them, "How will this lawsuit affect my business? What advice do you have for me to help my business to continue growing during this process?" You can get a sense of whether they have a good idea of business from questions they ask in return. For example, I'll ask about clients' current and future expansion plans, whether they've been involved in any other lawsuits, and how that has affected their business.

If they can't answer your questions, or they don't have any follow-up questions about your business, they probably don't understand or care about your business.

To get a sense of how well a prospective lawyer understands your business, you can ask: "Have you represented anyone in my industry? Have you worked in my industry? What do you know about my industry?"

Ask these hard questions early on. Don't wait until you're halfway through or close to the end to learn that your lawyer doesn't know anything about you or your business.

Lawyers should consider the specific needs of your business when setting a strategy. For example, if you have a dispute with a vendor or client, but you need them to continue doing business, you want the lawyer to understand that he can't do anything that would blow up the relationship.

Say it's a dispute with a key vendor—a good question might be, "Do you have alternative sources?" And if the answer is "no," then maybe you're not as aggressive. Maybe instead of going for the jugular, you go for a middle-of-the-road result that they're more likely to agree to, because you need this dispute to end quickly. You want to hire the lawyer who can take an aggressive approach when needed, but also knows when to take the tempered, political approach when appropriate.

But if you have other sources, and you're really upset, then you might want to go full steam ahead.

Another key question a lawyer should ask you is how long you can continue with the dispute or the lawsuit, based on your business and your budgetary limits.

Communication

It is important that a lawyer communicates clearly with their client. You want to know that they'll respond quickly, listen to your concerns, and explain things simply. And you can get a good sense of their communication the first time you discuss your case. Here is what to look for.

Can You Talk to Them?

Movies and TV series are filled with prickly, brilliant, off-putting lawyers. Now, I won't say you can't get good representation from a lawyer with poor communication skills. But you're more likely to get good representation with a lawyer who treats you with respect, listens to your questions, and offers clear answers and explanations.

What's the sense you get from a lawyer when you have a conversation with them? Are they easy to talk to? Approachable? Relatable? Do you feel they want to help you and know what needs to be done? Do you feel like they're giving you straight answers?

THE ENTREPRENEUR'S LEGAL PLAYBOOK

Or do they come across like car salesmen, pushing you to sign on the dotted line? Are they dismissive? Belittling? Rude?

Choose the lawyer you can comfortably talk to.

Do They Listen to You?

A lot of people don't really listen. This is especially true in "high-end" professions, like doctors and lawyers. There's this attitude of, "I already know what's best; I don't need you to tell me anything."

When you talk to a lawyer, make sure they're listening and that they respond in ways that show they hear—and care about—what you say. We've all been in conversations where you say something, and it's clear the other person is just waiting for their turn to speak. And when that turn comes, they say something unrelated to what you just said. If a lawyer you're considering hiring is doing that, you should keep looking.

Listening is a sign of respect, and if they're not showing you respect, it's hard to trust them.

Can They Answer Your Questions?

It's easy for someone to BS you if you ask surface-level questions. But when you ask them the deeper questions of the why and the how, you get a real sense of whether they know what they're talking about. So ask, "Why did you do that? How did you accomplish that—what did you do?" They may not be able to share all the specifics with you because of attorney-client privilege or some other reason. But you can ask for a general overview and get a deeper sense of how they handled things.

Additionally, you can ask how they would approach a case like yours. If they say, "Well, I can't tell you that; we will just have to see how this case goes, and who's involved," and they're very vague...they're probably not that good of a lawyer. Because from a simple conversation, a good lawyer will have at least some sense of how they would probably approach a case. Of course, they should tell you that things could change depending on what further information comes out, but they should be able to give you their overall sense of the matter and how they would approach it.

They should also be able to explain it in plain English. If they're explaining in legalese, so you can't really make sense of it, then you can expect them to continue doing that throughout the case, and you'll never really know what's happening.

And don't accept an answer like, "Don't worry about the details; I know how to handle this; leave it in my hands." Because if they don't or can't answer your questions, you have no way of telling if they really understand the case.

Can They Play Well with Others?

There's an art to being a lawyer. You need to have the respect of opposing counsel and know when to push and when to ease up.

In terms of judging a lawyer's character, figuring out how well they can engage in that push-and-pull is not easy, but there are clues to look for.

Some lawyers are real bulldogs. There are times when being very aggressive can work to your advantage, but a lawyer who never takes the measured approach is going to create problems.

You can get some sense of a lawyer's level of aggression from their demeanor and from the way they explain their results and strategies to you. If they're aggressive when speaking to you—yelling or acting insulted that you would ask questions instead of just taking their word for it—there's a good chance they're like that all the time, and that is not a good thing.

Of course, you also don't want a lawyer who is bumbling and fumbling and can't articulate their thoughts concisely. If you're not persuaded by that person, they probably won't be any better at persuading a jury or judge. If you don't feel much respect for them, there's a good chance that opposing counsel will feel the same way.

Do They Have Passion?

You want a lawyer who genuinely wants to get a great result, not one who is just treating your case as a boring legal chore they have to complete.

You can usually tell if people are passionate about what they do. Lawyers who like their job will be enthusiastic when they're talking to you about your case and how to handle it. They'll get excited when they tell you about their past results.

This is a bonus of asking questions—not only do you get answers, but you get a sense of the lawyer.

The Danger of Superficial Appeal

Of course, a lot of what I'm talking about requires some ability to judge character. That's not always easy, and sometimes if a lawyer has charisma and gravitas, you can be swept away.

Think about Tom Cruise. He has played the role of a lawyer multiple times. If you described your case to Tom Cruise, he could absolutely convince you that he could win it. He would exude confidence and charm. But of course, Tom Cruise has never practiced law, has no track record, and has no legal expertise at all—so he would be a terrible choice. Even if it's someone as impressive as Tom Cruise, you still need to do some research. You still have to ask, "Have you successfully handled cases like mine?"

Another mistake people make when hiring a lawyer is going with someone from their own culture—the same country, the same state, the same country club or networking group—even if that lawyer has no relevant experience. While culture can create a sense of comfort and a feeling that the lawyer gets you, a lawyer from your hometown who knows nothing about your business and has never worked on a case like yours is just a bad bet.

And while it's understandable for someone to choose a lawyer who speaks their native language if it would be difficult to communicate well otherwise, seeking out a lawyer just because they speak your language and know your culture severely limits your options. If you're from India, and you want an Indian lawyer who speaks Hindi, you probably won't have that many lawyers to choose from. So, you won't be as selective as you should be.

Researching Lawyers

Choosing a lawyer is a mixture of learning about them through conversation and learning about them through research. You can learn a lot about a lawyer with an online search.

Check Their Website and Online Presence

If a lawyer's website is a mess, that could just mean that they get so much business through referrals that they don't really need a good website. But it could be a red flag, and if they don't have a professionally designed, functional website, it should make you a little cautious.

If you google a lawyer, and there isn't much of anything about them on the Internet—no website, no social media presence, no photos—well, that's just odd. Sure, they might not be media-savvy, but I would need a lot of third-party validation and impressive references before considering this person is reliable and trustworthy.

Like any other business, lawyers get reviewed online, so that's a good way to see what people are saying about their experiences with that lawyer. Besides the usual business reviews through sites like Google, you can also look up a lawyer on the website avvo.com, which ranks lawyers based on their own algorithm.

Some lawyers' websites will tout the awards they have won—but be aware those aren't always as impressive as they sound. Many are pay-to-play and don't indicate real merit. I've been offered awards in areas I don't even practice in! So, if a lawyer lists an award, you might want to google it and see whether it has any real prestige or value.

How a Prospective Lawyer Should Talk to You

Recently, I met with someone with a high-value, out-of-state case with over a hundred million dollars in exposure. He was having concerns about his lawyers, who just didn't seem to really get it, even though they'd been practicing for decades. He felt like they were getting played by opposing counsel—that they weren't able to read the situation and get him the best result possible.

So, I looked at some of the facts and the issues, and I agreed with him that their approach didn't make sense to me. I told him, without asking for his take, what I thought. And he said, "That's exactly what I think."

His lawyers had been working on the case for eight months, but they weren't collaborative with the client, and they weren't telling him things that he should have known. Part of the reason they weren't really getting it was because they weren't fully communicating with their client—they had never asked how his business worked or how he got clients.

When he decided to bring me in as lead counsel on two related cases, I asked those questions they hadn't asked. And the answers helped me better understand what the damages argument should be and how to craft the strategy going forward.

I don't relate this as a way of claiming I am such an amazing lawyer. Instead, I just want you to understand what you can reasonably expect: A lawyer who listens to you and asks the questions necessary to put together an effective strategy. If you talk to a lawyer and don't feel he's that kind of lawyer, keep looking.

There are a lot of lawyers out there—don't settle for one you have doubts about, and don't be shy about asking questions or doing your due diligence before hiring. Choosing a lawyer can make or break your case, and the right lawyer can give you something that is priceless when you're dealing with legal issues while running your business: peace of mind.

CHAPTER 12

How Lawsuits Work

When you see cases on TV where someone gets sued, things jump pretty quickly from the initial conflict to the courtroom, where there are a lot of twists and turns and startling evidence that changes everything. But in the real world, less than 2 percent of lawsuits even reach trial, and when they do, it is only the final part of an often lengthy process.

So, I'm going to lay out how lawsuits proceed. There are three main parts to a lawsuit: filing, discovery, and the trial. And even after trial, you could keep going with motions and appeals.

However, from the point a lawsuit is filed, the whole process can end at any time, if the parties agree to settle. So, even as I lay out this whole process, which can go on for months or even years, keep in mind that everything can suddenly be over at any point in the process.

1: Filing the Lawsuit

A lawsuit is begun when someone files a complaint with either state or federal court, which will depend on where the case is located. Different courts have different timelines and deadlines. The plaintiff, meaning the person filing the complaint, gets to choose where they file the complaint and start the lawsuit. Sometimes a complaint can be filed in one of multiple places, and there are strategic considerations on how and when to file.

Sometimes you can properly file in one of several different venues, so you make a strategic decision based on that jurisdiction's laws, or how quickly your case can get to trial, or what the disclosure and other requirements are for that venue.

The filing of a lawsuit stops what's called the "statute of limitations." As mentioned, the analogy I like to use is it's like a game clock that's ticking down. And once the clock gets to zero, you essentially don't have the ability to bring your claim forward. But the way it works is that a series of facts can give rise to multiple potential claims, so they each can have a different statute of limitations.

A client also needs to coordinate with their attorney to see which statute of limitations apply to their case and their various claims, because as the game clock runs down to zero on each of them, the door to file those claims will shut forever.

While filing a lawsuit stops the game clock, sending a demand or negotiating with the other side does not. Often people will think,

"It must count for something that I'm negotiating with the other side, trying to work it out instead of bothering the court and spending all the time and money for a lawsuit." But that's not how it works. There are ways to pause the game clock, such as creating a valid and enforceable tolling agreement that says that the game clock stops while you work things out. But by default, the clock is running.

Opponents will sometimes try to run out your game clock. Insurance companies do this all the time, especially with people who don't have attorneys. They'll just keep the conversation going, making it seem like they want to settle. They'll say, "We just need to look at these documents; we're just waiting on something." And then once the clock runs out, they say, "Oh, sorry. Your time to file a claim has run out, so now we value your claim at zero dollars."

We've had people come to us and say, "We were discussing it with the insurance company or with the other side." They'd say they would get us this information and that information, and that they just needed a little bit more time until, suddenly, the statute ran out.

If the statute of limitations runs out, that's it. There are limited exceptions to this, but they are rarely applicable. So, it's very important to be aware of where the game clock is at all times.

2: Discovery

Discovery is where you get to ask the other side for information, and they get to ask you for information. You can also try to get information from third parties, meaning people who aren't directly involved in the lawsuit.

On TV, discovery usually consists of a montage of lawyers reading documents the night before a trial, with almost all the real lawyering happening in court. But discovery is your opportunity to build your case—it is what sets your case up for success or failure.

In real trials, there isn't a Perry Mason or Matlock moment, where evidence just pops up at the last second and blows the case apart. You're not supposed to surprise the other side with something they are unable to prepare for—instead, you are typically required to figure out your case beforehand, and you do that through strategic discovery. So, a good discovery plan is critical. You need information—and you need to know where you're going to get that information, how you're going to get it, and who has the information you need.

There are a few different ways to get the information you need. There are "requests for production," where you ask the other side to produce certain documents or information for you, such as emails, contracts, letters, text messages, and other kinds of communication. Then there's "requests for admission," where you're asking the other side to admit certain facts as true or not true. The purpose of requests for admission is to narrow the factual issues for trial.

Then, there are "interrogatories," which involve broader, more open-ended questions—for example, "Please state all facts supporting the claim that Jack Black breached this contract." They have to provide a list, and if they leave something off of that list, you can exclude that evidence at trial. Because you're not supposed to withhold information from the other side and then try to sandbag them at trial. However, the other side will often try to withhold sensitive or damaging information, which is why being proactive in discovery is essential.

If the lawyer doesn't know the rules, doesn't know the game, and doesn't object or set the groundwork for the later move, then you're out of luck. This is why it's so important to have somebody who knows what they're doing and who's played the entirety of the game before—not just parts of it.

Opposing attorneys will absolutely try and sandbag you throughout the process, but there are safeguards in place if you know to use them. For example, as long as you've made the proper objections at trial, then you're more likely to win an appeal because you can say, "Look, I raised this issue." Every time you see a TV lawyer present startling, last-minute evidence that upends the case, say to yourself, "That will be thrown out on appeal."

When you ask the other side questions in writing, that's called "written discovery," where answers are submitted that attorneys can help shape. They've usually got thirty days to send you the responses, which will likely be a combination of objections and half-answers, and then you've got to meet and confer. Once they finally answer your questions, you submit follow-up questions that go through the same process. This is why written discovery can take months. It's a long and arduous process.

"Depositions" allow you to have face-to-face, real-time conversations with those involved, either in person or via remote conferencing software like Zoom, which moves much faster. Lawyers aren't supposed to interfere in the conversation, even though they sometimes do, but the benefit is you can ask follow-up questions immediately. Depositions are the fastest way to get your questions answered, but you don't want to do everything through depositions because, for one thing, they are very expensive. For a day-long deposition, which is about seven hours long, the court reporter alone will probably bill over three thousand dollars. Add in attorney's fees, and you've probably got a ten-thousand-dollar day.

Good lawyers make a strategic decision when it comes to choosing written discovery versus deposition. Written discovery will make more sense for things like, "Give me all of the documents that state this." Or, when it comes to certain kinds of legal contention questions like, "Do you contend that my client breached this contract?" They can often be handled initially through written discovery. Targeted follow-up questions—particularly those you expect the other side will struggle to answer without their attorney's guidance—are often best reserved for the deposition.

So, usually the ideal strategy is to use written questions to get the high-level information that you'll need when asking more details at a deposition. Ideally, you want to get as much of the documents and information that you can get before the deposition. Because even though people under deposition take an oath to tell the truth, time and time again I've seen them avoid as much of the truth as they can get away with. So, I always want to make sure that I've got the backup and the evidence *before* the deposition to help set the stage.

A deposition is also where things get tied together. Strategically, these are like chess pieces on a chess board. When moved effectively and efficiently, they set the stage for a more efficient outcome.

I think this is where a lot of attorneys get it wrong—they don't move the pieces efficiently or effectively, which ends up costing their clients a lot more money than it should. The best attorneys look at the whole chess board and think about moves to maximize the efficiency of how they get the information. The best lawyers maximize the "return on investment" for their client's fees.

How a Deposition Won a Case

A lot of times, cases are made or broken during discovery. A good job in discovery will set the path forward for the trial where you present all the information and the evidence you have gathered.

If your case has worked out correctly in discovery, it will usually not have to go to trial at all, because it will become increasingly obvious that one side's case is stronger, pushing the other side to settle.

In fact, while the internal intention of discovery is to get to the objective truth and determine the pros and cons of your client's case, the external intention is to show the other side why you're going to win at trial. So, you push on all the evidence and information that shows the other side that their case is weak. You want them to feel they are better off settling versus blowing their time and money on a trial they are almost certain to lose.

For example, I had a client who had built a successful real estate business with her boyfriend, starting out with money provided by my client. After they broke up, they were still 50/50 owners according to their partnership agreement. They had used the online service LegalZoom to draw up a fairly generic agreement, which is a common mistake people make when starting a business.

Even though she was the only one who had put in money, her ex claimed he was entitled to at least half the value of the real estate, which was close to four million, based on the partnership agreement. My client had tried to settle it before filing the lawsuit against him, but he didn't want to resolve it, so it went into litigation.

He accused her of self-dealing by giving her other company favorable leases for these properties, and of misreporting financials for tax purposes. So, he had a number of what his 50 percent was valued at and said any lower value she presented was the result of her having mishandled the financials for the properties in question. There were leases in place that were below market value and were inappropriate, and taxes had not been filed on time.

But when I deposed him, he admitted to being the Chief Financial Officer for the business—who was supposed to be looking after the numbers and the finances—and admitted that he was the one who signed off on the tax returns. So, the numbers he contended were inaccurate had ultimately been his responsibility. I asked him, "If there were issues with the leasing, as Chief Financial Officer, weren't they your responsibility?""

Essentially, all of the arguments he'd made about what my client had done wrong turned out to be the result of his own negligence, and the amount of damages he'd claimed were actually his responsibility, not hers.

He got very nervous during the deposition. He took a break, then said he didn't want to continue. I kept pressing for another deposition, with his lawyers saying he couldn't participate because he wasn't feeling well. And as I kept pushing for dates, they then wanted to resolve the case.

We ended up settling the case within a week or two after that deposition. In the settlement, he got a small fraction of what he was originally contending he was owed. In fact, he got much less than what my client had offered him before we filed the lawsuit.

So, it was a very good result for my client, and one that resolved long before trial. However, as I said before, about 2 percent of cases do end up going to trial, so you still want to be mentally prepared for how trial works.

3: The Trial

Every once in a while, a lawsuit makes it all the way to the trial stage.

On TV, the trial, which is the presentation of your case to a judge or arbitrator or jury, is everything. That's the stuff that seems sexy and exciting. But all the groundwork laid during discovery sets the basis for a successful trial.

Trials vary. There are bench trials, where the case is decided by the judge, and there are jury trials. In jury trials, you need a unanimous verdict in federal court, but that's not always the case in state court. For example, in California, you need nine out of twelve jurors to vote in your favor as the plaintiff to win.

There are strategic considerations in whether to file in federal or state court, and whether to request a bench trial or a jury trial. Both sides have a say on whether or not there's a jury—in the U.S., everyone has the right to a jury trial, so if one side wants one, that's what happens.

Jurors come in with their own life experience, and part of the beauty of the jury system is to take a cross-section of the community and have them decide what's right and wrong based on the law.

The challenge is in how well you explain things. Statistically, the average juror has a high school education, so it's critical to have a lawyer who can simplify it all and keep it interesting. Evidence and information must be provided in a way that makes people want to pay attention, because in today's social media age, our attention span is short. You have to be able to get in, get their attention, keep it, make your point so they understand it, and get out. And ultimately, you've got to present it all in a way that makes them want to vote for you and for your client.

There are a number of factors and a lot of psychology that goes into that presentation. Humans are tribal, and in any group, you're likely to see two or three leaders emerge. So, when presenting information, you really want to understand who will have the most influence over the way the jurors accesses that information.

Jury Selection

A trial is a chess match, and there are a number of moves you can make during jury selection. Asking questions is not simply about revealing bias—you can also use your questions to frame the case to get jurors thinking in a particular way.

Lawyers have the ability to strike jurors for cause, such as clear bias. They also have peremptory challenges, where you can strike a juror without giving a reason, but those are limited, so you want to show cause as much as you can.

There's an art to getting somebody to admit that they're biased, because even the most biased people will tell you they are fair and objective. But the reality is, everybody walks into that courtroom with their own biases, so the real question is: "How biased are they?"

You have to ask yourself, "Is this an acceptable level of bias? Can they look at these facts and make a decision with relative objectivity? Or are they going to make the decision based on things that aren't presented at trial?" Because the whole idea is that they're supposed to make a decision based on the evidence that's presented at trial.

Considerations When Choosing Between a Jury and a Bench Trial

A lot of people like the idea of a jury trial, but for the vast majority of business cases, you'll want to have the judge decide.

For one thing, juries add a lot of time and expense to the trial. There's the process of gathering the jury and giving them the instructions. In the morning, jurors file in and take time finding their seats. There are breaks, which include time waiting for the inevitable stragglers. A juror might get sick or injured, and the whole case can slow down.

Jurors are also likely to lack interest in complicated contractual matters or dense financial calculations, and the last thing you want is a case decided by people who are tuned out. For cases like that, you want a bench trial or to use an arbitrator.

Judges and arbitrators are likely to be able to keep focused on complex issues, but you still need to keep your audience in mind. For example, if you try a case with a lot of technological elements, and the judge is struggling with the conferencing technology, you have to make sure you present the technological elements simply, even though you'll be able to speak on the actual legal matters at a higher level.

Another big consideration on whether you want a jury trial is how likable your client is. That's more likely to be a factor for a jury than a judge. So, if you've got a client who is technically correct but just very off-putting, inarticulate, or hard to understand because of a heavy accent, then they're not going to present as well. And if the other side has a very charismatic, charming speaker who's fun to listen to, a jury could get lost in that.

How Juries Make Decisions

In our normal lives, we make decisions based on how things seem. Does this guy sound trustworthy? Do I think he's making sense?

That's why juries are more likely than a judge or an arbitrator to make decisions based on things that aren't directly at issue.

That's natural, because jurors don't sit in judgment professionally. They don't have a judge's experience of going into a court, putting biases aside, and just basing their decisions entirely on the evidence.

But often we judge whether someone is making sense based more on the way they explain things than on the underlying logic or how technically correct they are. That's why it's important when deciding whether you want a jury trial to look at the complexity of the subject matter and ask yourself, "How likely is it that the jury will pay attention?"

When I was a baby lawyer trying my very first case, the other side brought in some heavy legal guns. First, there was a sharp lawyer who had been practicing as long as I'd been alive. Then, as trial approached, the other side brought in a second lawyer, who was even better than the first guy, to help try this case against me. I didn't know anything about him, so I asked on a legal listserv and got comments like, "They must be concerned about this case because you don't bring in this guy for just any case. This guy charges a lot of money for cases, and he's very, very well-known in the community." And I understood why, because he was very likable and charismatic.

This was a high-value case with a lot of exposure on both sides. It was a serious case, and I was trying it on a shoestring budget, so I didn't have the funds for a jury consultant or a jury focus group where you hire people at random to represent the jury and get their feedback on the strengths and weaknesses in your case.

So, in order to get a sense of how the sort of people who might wind up on a jury would react to the case, I went to the central bus hub in Los Angeles to get their take. I knew what seemed important to me as a lawyer, but I wanted to know what non-lawyers thought in case I had to present to a jury. The feedback I received was remarkable and incredibly helpful. It helped me see things, both positive and negative, in the case in slightly different ways.

For example, one African-American woman said, "It just sounds to me like a couple of old, rich white guys fighting over a bunch of money when I can't even afford to pay my bills."

I didn't tell her that. I didn't tell her the race of anybody involved in the case. But she was absolutely right. She added, "I can't even pay my rent. Nobody came and gave me any money. And this guy, your client, has got all this money to spend on this, and now I gotta take time off work to come listen to his case?"

That's when I decided that it was going to be a bench trial.

You have to remember that people on the jury have lives. They're not getting paid what they're losing from work to be there. It's usually only about twenty bucks a day, depending on where the trial is. So, it's a very real hardship for many of them.

So, while my clients might believe they have a righteous case and were severely wronged, the jurors are going to be asking, "Is this really worth my time?" Because if you have a case that the average juror is going to think of as a stupid waste of their time,

THE ENTREPRENEUR'S LEGAL PLAYBOOK

then you're better off going to a judge or an arbitrator who's getting paid to be there. Because it's their job to hear the facts and then make a decision.

Advantages of a Bench Trial

The bench trial is when you get to just try it straight to a judge. You typically get more time per day, because there's no jury-wrangling and you have no jury instructions. That means a bench trial will usually only be about 10 to 20 percent of the length of a jury trial and will cost much less to take through trial. If you have a very unemotional, unsexy case about numbers and money that's full of facts and figures, that's probably going to be better for a judge or an arbitrator than a jury.

If it's a sexy, exciting case with juicy facts, then you might want a jury. For example, when Ed Sheeran was sued over copyright infringement issues, he got on the stand and started playing songs while explaining how a lot of major pop songs are essentially different combinations of the same four chords. So, you've got Ed Sheeren on the stand singing songs and playing music, saying, "I didn't copy somebody else's chords; this is just how pop music works." For Ed Sheeran, that's a good case to take in front of a jury. Because a jury is going to be able to say, "Yes, that sounds similar," or "No, that sounds different." They'll say, "What Ed Sheeran said makes sense to me," and having Ed Sheeran put on a mini show from the witness stand is extremely entertaining.

But let's say it was a pure royalty dispute, where Ed Sheeran hadn't been paid a certain amount of money for certain songs that have been streamed from Spotify. Then you're just talking pure numbers with no performance aspect to it, so you'd probably be better off with a judge or an arbitrator that is comfortable adjudicating financial cases.

How Long Do Trials Take?

The length of a trial varies. Jury trials often take two to three times longer than bench trials. The length of a case is also determined by the number of facts and witnesses you've got. Some cases are resolved in a day or two, while others can go on for weeks or months. Some trials will drag on for more than a year.

It can get very complex and time-consuming, depending on how many witnesses there are, how much evidence there is, and everything you have to go through. Sometimes you have a lot of witnesses.

People want you to respect their time, which is why you want to make the best, most compelling argument you can for your client and then be done. If you're just hammering on some point you've already made multiple times, they won't appreciate that. They could even hold it against you. So, you also have to be aware of scheduling and how long it's going to take.

During discovery is when you figure a lot of this out. Do you need to present these ten documents, or does this one document do everything those ten would do? You find a way to take everything you've got and state it concisely so that people get it. You want to make it memorable. A classic example is the O.J. Simpson trial. It went on for over a year. There was so much evidence, so many documents, so many photos and testimonies. Then, right at the end, Johnny Cochran brilliantly summarized the entire case as, "If the glove don't fit, you must acquit." A year's plus worth of testimony and trial days into that one sentence—it was brilliant. The quote was so brilliant that it instantly became a part of pop culture and is still mentioned today, decades after that trial.

That's the art of great lawyering: the ability to communicate simply and clearly so people get it.

Appeals, Post-Trial Motions, and Settlement

Sooner or later, the trial will reach the end with a "verdict" in the case of a jury, or a "decision" in the case of a judge or arbitrator. But that doesn't necessarily mean you're done.

First, there are post-trial motions you can make. For example, you can ask to simply have a jury's verdict overturned, because the jury disregarded the law or made some other mistake. You can also ask for a new trial if you feel you did not get a fair trial.

You can also appeal any issues they think were incorrectly decided. Although, if you used an arbitrator, your appeal options are very limited.

The appeal process is lengthy, time-consuming, and expensive, so sometimes just the threat of an appeal is enough to make one side compromise or further negotiate on payment. For both sides, it can make sense to accept a lesser number rather than go through an appeal. Part of it depends on how great a chance you think there is that the appeal is successful. And of course, you want to persuade the other side that the appeal will not come out in their favor.

When to Settle

I mentioned at the start of this chapter that, at any time during this process, everything can just stop if the parties agree to a settlement. If they can come to an agreement on their own, then there is no need to continue the lawsuit process.

In every lawsuit, there's an ideal time to settle. The trick is to stay aware of the relative strengths of risk and reward. When the risk starts closing in on or exceeding the reward, or when expenses such as attorney's fees begin to outweigh your possible recovery, a settlement usually becomes the best option. It's important for the attorney handling the case to be able to understand and explain these calculations to the client so that they can make an informed decision.

The less money that's at issue in the case, the sooner that point of settlement has to be. Because there is less opportunity for lawyers to create real value in a small-value case. But there are other factors, and sometimes you need more information just to get a clearer picture of the value of a case.

If you have a customer with unpaid invoices, you know they owe you money, you know when the invoices went out, and you know what the invoices were for. But you may not know why your customer hasn't paid. They may just be ducking your calls, but maybe they're disappointed in your work. Maybe they don't have the money. Or maybe they're just trying to get out of paying because they're that sort of customer.

You can't know how worthwhile a lawsuit would be without answers to these questions, but getting those answers may involve time and expense.

For example, we've been working through a case that involves highly complex coding. A company has been using software developed by my client. The company has gone from no users and no revenue to tens of thousands of users and tens of millions of dollars in revenue, but they haven't paid my client's invoices for the services rendered that resulted in the coding that created the tens of millions of dollars in annual revenue. They owe my client hundreds of thousands of dollars in unpaid coding fees.

The other side contends that the software is faulty and doesn't live up to the industry standard. That raises the questions: "What is the industry standard for something like this? What was reasonable to expect?" Sorting through that is going to be complicated and expensive, because it's not perfectly clear at this moment exactly what the "objective industry standard" is.

With my client claiming his software is up to the industry standard, and the other side saying it isn't, we need to hire experts who understand the industry standard before we can have an understanding of the pros and cons of each side's arguments.

Those experts may say, "This is fully up to industry standard." Or they may say, "This was almost up to industry standard, but it was missing elements X, Y, and Z," and the value of those features is, let's say twenty thousand dollars. In the first case, we're suing for the hundreds of thousands of dollars they owe, and in the second case, we're suing for hundreds of thousands of dollars less than twenty thousand dollars, assuming the features were missing. Either way, a lawsuit makes sense in that scenario.

But what if the expert comes in and says, "This isn't even close to the industry standard—it's not at all valuable." Given that information, pursuing the case might be a bad idea.

But it often takes time and expense to get to the point where you can make that determination. If you don't have the information, you have to spend time and money to get it before you can make an informed decision.

Now, sometimes it's not just about the money, it's a matter of principle. But most of the time it's about money. It's a civil suit. No one's going to jail at the end of it. So, even though there can be a sense of personal satisfaction in winning a lawsuit even if you lose money on it, the vast majority of clients want it to make financial sense. They want to see a financial recovery in excess of the time and money they spent. I call that the "return on investment." What multiples are clients getting above and beyond what they spend in attorney's fees?

That is why it is important to make sure your lawyer understands when pursuing a lawsuit makes financial sense, and when a lawsuit may have reached the tipping point where pursuing it no longer makes financial sense.

CHAPTER 13

Always Focus on the Outcome

"Within every adversity is an equal or greater benefit. Within every problem is an opportunity. Even in the knocks of life, we can find great gifts." —Napoleon Hill

You might fantasize about a perfect entrepreneurial life where you don't face any problems or adversity, but the truth is the exact opposite. Entrepreneurship is an endless series of problems and challenges that you have to overcome.

To overcome these challenges, you've got to show up as a better version of yourself each time. Every challenge will result in a better you.

Maybe you're currently facing a lawsuit that has the potential to bankrupt you and destroy your business. How do you overcome this obstacle or this problem? You need to:

1. Find the right help to overcome the challenge,

2. Attain the right knowledge to understand how to best overcome that challenge,

3. Persevere through the challenges, knowing that's what entrepreneurship really is.

You will never reach a point where you have no more problems or challenges. But if you handle these issues in the right way, you can create opportunities that you would not have otherwise seen. And when you overcome an obstacle or a challenge, or solve a problem, you come out of it as a better problem-solver. Now, if you face that problem again, it'll be easier for you to navigate, because you've got more of the knowledge and information and experience you need to be able to overcome other, bigger challenges.

The Outcome

If you ask people what outcome they would hope for when facing a challenge, it would be essentially, "And then they lived happily ever after." No more problems. But that's impossible outside of a fairy tale. I think a lot of people believe or want to believe that that's how it is, but that is not reality.

So, when facing a challenge, always focus on the real outcome—which is, ultimately, a better version of you. For each problem, that's the outcome to focus on.

Start by asking yourself: What's the current outcome for this issue? And then ask yourself: No matter what the outcome, how will

ALWAYS FOCUS ON THE OUTCOME

this help me become a better businessperson or a better leader? Focus on that endgame of becoming a better person. Because without these challenges, you wouldn't have that opportunity.

And as you become a better you, each challenge becomes a step towards the final outcome of the legacy you've built. You want that to be great.

And that's what this journey is about. This journey of entrepreneurship is exactly that—building your business, building your legacy, building yourself to become that highest and best version of yourself that you can possibly be. And all the challenges and adversity you face, the struggles you overcome, will take you step by step to the final outcome of your business and your legacy.

The Celebrity Bar Break-In

I have a client who owns a famous celebrity hotspot in Hollywood.

In 2020, he started getting worried about how his bar could be affected by the political unrest of COVID and the George Floyd protests. Worried about the possibility of rioting and looting, he asked his broker to get an insurance policy to protect his bar and the millions of dollars he had put into it for improvements. His broker assured him he had done as requested, and that the policy had been issued. My client felt safer after that.

While the bar was shut down during COVID, there were a series of break-ins at his place. He wasn't checking up on it that often, and the robbers somehow circumvented the alarm when they cut through his wall. They boldly went in, breaking off copper pipes and anything else that could be sold for scrap. They literally started taking pieces out of his business and selling them on the street.

By the time he returned, there was a lot of damage—hundreds of thousands of dollars at a minimum, although the exact number was disputed. He needed to rebuild his bar and get it back open, since he was losing money every day it was closed.

But the broker who said that he had purchased the insurance policy hadn't, although he claimed that he genuinely believed at the time that he had. He owned up that it was his mistake, but he didn't have the kind of money to make it right. However, he did have an Errors and Omissions policy, which is like a malpractice policy for insurance brokers.

But instead of immediately covering the damages, the insurance company created all kinds of arguments and issues, delaying paying out for the rebuilding of the property. My client also had some issues with his other businesses that all stemmed from COVID, so things were tight financially, and nobody was willing to give him a loan to rebuild the bar.

So, my client's bar was shut down, and he couldn't rebuild it. He couldn't do anything with it. He was teetering on potentially losing the bar and all the money he had put into this place. This situation was costing him a lot in terms of attorney's fees, because this dispute with the insurance company went on for three years.

So naturally, my client was very upset by all this.

But ultimately, we got the case settled for far more than what anybody had expected was possible when we started.

But that wasn't all.

My client hadn't gotten along well with his landlord, and he wanted to just buy the property from him. But the landlord never wanted to sell. He had valuable property in Hollywood, so he saw it as a gold mine with a value that would always increase.

But the landlord was getting older; there were issues with the property, and now it had been trashed by drug addicts and wasn't producing income because the bar was shut down. The cleanup process was going to be time-consuming and expensive. So suddenly, he was open to selling.

My client not only got the money to fix the bar but was able to purchase the property, because he was able to repair it for less than the overall insurance proceeds. That purchase probably wouldn't have happened if not for those break-ins and all the headaches they'd created for the landlord, who didn't want to deal with it.

So, that tragedy turned into something positive. My client got the money to rebuild his bar, got a little extra money even after rebuilding and paying for his attorney's fees, and got a chance to buy the property that he'd wanted for years.

So yes, he had a couple of really terrible years. But now, he is in a better position than he was before everything went south. That was his outcome. That is what you want to focus on when things are going bad—that you can do more than just survive this challenge. Adversity can actually take you further in your entrepreneurial evolution.

Ultimately, your goal isn't just to sidestep problems—it's to build a business that thrives, evolves, and leaves a lasting legacy. I hope this book offers insights to help you prepare for and confidently navigate both legal challenges and broader entrepreneurial crises on your journey of growth and success.

About the Author

Parag L. Amin is a litigator, trial attorney, and entrepreneur dedicated to helping others protect their businesses, livelihoods, and legacies. His journey into law was shaped by personal experience - after watching his father lose his life's savings and entrepreneurial dreams to a dishonest businessman, Parag committed himself to fighting for people facing similar challenges. Over the course of his career, he has recovered more than $280 million for his clients and successfully represented public figures, small businesses, and individuals in high-stakes disputes.

Parag has been a featured legal and business analyst on ABC, CBS, Fox, NBC, and KTLA, and has been quoted in the L.A. Times, L.A. Weekly, and Rolling Stone. He has been named a SuperLawyers Rising Star every year since 2017 - an honor given to just 2.5% of attorneys based on peer recognition and excellence in practice. The L.A. Times has also recognized him as a Legal Visionary.

When he's not advocating for clients, Parag enjoys time with his family, friends, and dog, often outdoors or at the beach seeking his next adventure.

Contact Information & Links

www.ingramcontent.com/pod-product-compliance
Lightning Source LLC
Chambersburg PA
CBHW022039190326
41520CB00008B/639